SELECTED POEMS

CHARLOTTE BRONTË (1816-1855) is best known for her novels, *Jane Eyre* (1847), *Shirley* (1849), *Villette* (1853) and *The Professor* (1857). A collection of poems by Charlotte and her sisters Emily and Anne was published in 1846.

EMILY BRONTË (1818-1848) is best known for her novel *Wuthering Heights* (1847).

ANNE BRONTË (1820-1849) is best known for her novel *The Tenant of Wildfell Hall* (1848).

STEVIE DAVIES is a literary critic, novelist, historian and biographer. She was elected a Fellow of the Royal Society of Literature in 1998, and now works as the Royal Literary Fund Writing Fellow at the University of Wales in Swansea, her home town. She taught English Literature at Manchester University before becoming a full-time author in 1984. She has written four distinguished books on Emily Brontë and edited Anne Brontë's *The Tenant of Wildfell Hall* for Penguin Classics. Her history of the seventeenth century, *A Century of Troubles* (2001), accompanied a Channel 4 TV series. Stevie Davies' first novel, *Boy Blue*, won the Fawcett Prize in 1989 and her latest novel, *The Element of Water* (Women's Press, 2001) was longlisted for the Booker Prize.

FyfieldBooks present poetry and prose by great as well as sometimes overlooked writers from British and Continental literatures. Clean texts at affordable prices, FyfieldBooks make available authors whose works endure within our literary tradition.

The series takes its name from the Fyfield elm mentioned in Matthew Arnold's 'The Scholar Gypsy' and in his 'Thyrsis'. The elm stood close to the building in which the Fyfield series was first conceived in 1971.

> *Roam on! The light we sought is shining still.*
> *Dost thou ask proof? Our tree yet crowns the hill,*
> *Our Scholar travels yet the loved hill-side*

from 'Thyrsis'

THE BRONTË SISTERS

Selected Poems

Edited with an introduction by
STEVIE DAVIES

Fyfield*Books*

CARCANET

First published in Great Britain
in 1976 by
Carcanet Press Limited
4th Floor, Conavon Court
12–16 Blackfriars Street
Manchester M3 5BQ

This impression 2002

A CIP catalogue record for this book
is available from the British Library

ISBN 0 85635 131 8

The publisher acknowledges financial
assistance from the Arts Council of England

Printed and bound in England by SRP Ltd, Exeter

To the dear memory of my Father

CONTENTS

7

PREFACE

My text of the poems by Charlotte and Anne Brontë is based on the Shakespeare Head edition of *The Poems of Charlotte Brontë and Patrick Branwell Brontë* and *The Poems of Emily Jane Brontë and Anne Brontë* (Oxford, 1934), edited by T. J. Wise and J. A. Symington. However, for the poems of Emily Jane Brontë, I have used C. W. Hatfield's invaluable edition of *The Complete Poems of Emily Jane Brontë* (New York, 1941). Of the wealth of Brontë scholarship, I must particularly mention my debt to F. E. Ratchford's reconstruction of the Gondal and Angrian stories in *The Brontës' Web of Childhood* (New York, 1941) and to W. Gérin's *Charlotte Brontë: The Evolution of Genius* (Oxford, 1967).

I should like to thank Rosalie Wilkins for her constant encouragement. And I am deeply grateful to Douglas Brooks for all his kindness, especially in advising me on the preparation of the notes.

Stevie Davies
Manchester

INTRODUCTION

The Brontës as Poets

Charlotte, Emily and Anne Brontë are generally far better known as novelists than poets. Charlotte's *Jane Eyre* and Emily's *Wuthering Heights* are the masterpieces everyone still recalls from childhood, and they hold something of the haunting quality of having long been assimilated into one's personal history. The lives of the three have likewise entered the collective consciousness, which has proceeded to mythologize them, so that the village where they lived, Haworth in Yorkshire, is the destination of hosts of visitors to the north of England. Haworth itself clusters around that century-old myth: its cafés, streets and souvenir shops bear their name and all its signposts seem to point in their direction.

There are various consequences of the perpetuation of their bleak and romantic story as a kind of folk-memory. First, their names have become a kind of sentimental public property, and interest in their nature as opposed to their work takes on the character of an assault. It is not only that the tiny parsonage at Haworth resounds with the footsteps of the curious — a fact that would have appalled the sisters as a nightmare incursion on their reserve. There are also the biographical works which prodigiously swell Brontë criticism, not to mention the whimsical plays and novels, whose protagonist is less likely to be the individual Brontë than the consumption that made off with her. It is often assumed that their whole lives are important only as a prelude to those heartrendingly early deaths.

In the hierarchy created by romantic taste, therefore, the lives come first, the novels (as an index to those lives) second, and the poems last, a condition which has changed little since *The Poems of Currer, Ellis and Acton Bell* were received in 1846 by an indifferent public, which could not be persuaded into buying more than a total of two copies. The edition had later to be destroyed as unsaleable. Yet none of the Brontës is a negligible poet, and Emily is a great one. They were Romantic in inspiration, writing both passionate confessional verse and poetry of the pure imagination. Certain themes are common to all three. They contemplate the idea of liberty,

9

pursuing and analysing it obsessively; they explore the nature of solitude; they write numerous love poems and harbour the myth of a lost Paradise. For each the imagination was the noblest faculty human nature possessed, and Emily's poem, 'Imagination', is one of the most powerful defences of the irrational ever written.

A certain formality of poetic technique was also shared. One could wish that the Brontës had been less captivated by regular metrical form to express their vision, less subject to the need to rhyme everything in sight. Lack of structural variety is linked to a tendency to repetitive vocabulary and ideas. Their favourite word seems to be 'drear' or 'dreary', which can be applied to anything at all, and is, liberally. Dungeons are particularly 'drear', so is sorrow, mortality, memory, words, rooms, graves, ghosts and innumerable other phenomena. 'Anguish', 'despair' and being 'desolate' are also popular with all three poets, but the word regarded with deepest affection by them is undoubtedly 'liberty'. Poems in which one of these terms, or a combination, is lacking, are rare, and yet this thematic limitation is more than compensated for by the intensity of the feeling which informs their work.

Interpretation of shared themes differs significantly: each poet expresses a unique vision and personality. Read in conjunction with the novels, the poems movingly elucidate the ideas on which each narrative revolves. Charlotte Brontë's Lucy Snowe in *Villette* is acting out the retreat into her own injured solitude as a result of blended sensitivity and physical unattractiveness that Charlotte Brontë in her poem 'Reason' stoically laments in herself. Emily Brontë's visionary poems, where she celebrates the spirit's escape from the fetters of the material world into union with its source, represent the kind of experience which in *Wuthering Heights* takes the form of Heathcliff's struggle to consummate his affinity with Catherine Linton in death. And Anne Brontë's denunciation in *The Tenant of Wildfell Hall* of the orthodox Christian God who is merciless enough to damn the disobedient, is echoed in a poem like 'A Word to the "Elect" ' which is fierce with distaste for the punitive God of the Calvinists.

The poems are also full of surprises, which often force one to reassess the character of the individual poet. According to the conventional stereotype, Charlotte confounded passion in reason; Emily confounded reason in passion; Anne, lamblike, had a gentle knowledge of both. The poems themselves, however, reveal how far each personality contained its own opposite. Charlotte Brontë, celebrating at the mighty age of fourteen the delights of bacchic feasting and alcohol in her Angrian poem, 'Written upon the Occasion of the Dinner Given to the Literati of the Glasstown', and busy creating immoral, seductive heroes like Zamorna, is far from the Charlotte Brontë of adulthood who rather inclined to be prudish and to disapprove of the sardonic violence of Emily's favourite heroes. Anne, too, yields many surprises. In Charlotte's opinion, Anne was a mild person of a domesticated spirit who needed fostering and protection from stronger beings such as herself. Charlotte thought the violence of Anne's second novel, *The Tenant of Wildfell Hall*, out of character for Anne, and fervently wished that her little sister had not coerced herself into writing it. But Anne and Emily, sharing their youthful fantasy world of Gondal, where civil war, political intrigue and sexual exploits were everyday occurrences, had fabricated for themselves a brutally anarchic universe which belonged just as much to Anne's as to Emily's imagination. This is evidenced by the strength of some of Anne's lyrics evolving out of the Gondal saga, such as the savagely beautiful poem on liberty, 'Song' ('We know where deepest lies the snow'). The gentleness of Anne's yearning love of God, and her fear of exile from him, has its converse in the adventure of the Gondal poems. By contrast, it is perhaps slightly unexpected to find how gentle Emily Brontë can be, for all the rebellion and defiance which characterize her most familiar mood. There is a great tenderness and simplicity in the elegies and farewell poems she wrote for her Gondal characters.

My selection, then, attempts to give some idea of the variety of thought and feeling within each author's work and of the way in which the sisters' poems parallel and reflect one another. I have also included those poems which seem to me crucial to an understanding of the themes of the novels.

Charlotte Brontë

Of the sisters, Charlotte is most clearly a novelist before she is a poet: the formal requirements of poetry inhibit her. For Charlotte, the poem's structure seems to represent a kind of pre-existing box into which you pack ideas, rather than the organic consequence of those ideas. Poeticism and archaism exert a magnetic pull on her, normal word order craves inversion (normally in response to the exigencies of rhyme), adjectives flower in every crevice of the verse and whole stanzas are choked with lists of Personalized Abstractions. She presides over her poetry with a certain solemnity and lack of humour.

Yet alongside this technical insecurity there is much that is moving. The main burden of her best poetry, as of the novels, is the expression of what it is like to live in a world where every other creature seems to enjoy companionship except oneself. This can take the form of a yearning for lost childhood as in the first part of 'The Teacher's Monologue', or a lament for the loneliness that is caused by physical plainness, which neither stoic rationality nor escape into fantasy can alleviate. While Emily Brontë's poems celebrate the mutinies of the moral or spiritual exile and Anne's rehearse the predicament of the soul forsaken by God, Charlotte's turn upon the theme of the disqualification of the ugly in a world dominated by the beautiful.

She is, in the poems, her own heroine, fulfilling a similar role to the heroines of *Jane Eyre* and *Villette*. Jane Eyre wistfully observes the beautiful and the rich at Thornfield Hall, an élite who appear to reside at the centre of the turning world, but ultimately it is she who receives the rewards of passion combined with moral beauty. Lucy Snowe in Charlotte's later, more pessimistic novel, *Villette*, homeless and cut off from love by the plainness of her face and by the coldness which selfconsciousness has bred in her, also looks on grimly from the edge of life, longing for a passion which ultimately eludes her. A poem of 1845 beginning 'Unloved I love, unwept I weep' renders in that first line alone an account of the crucial fact of Charlotte Brontë's existence with which the poetry and novels are a sustained attempt to come to terms.

There were two possible ways of doing this: the first might be called the Angrian solution. If a brighter and more magical reality could be substituted for the dreariness of everyday life, that fantasy might constitute a fulfilling alternative world. Angria was passion, warfare and all sorts of delectable emotions, and she continued to resort to it well into adult life. Its role can perhaps best be understood through study of her 1835 poem, 'Retrospection'. In essence it is a poem about symbolism, defining the relationship between 'real' and 'imaginary' worlds but casting doubt upon a common-sense interpretation of these concepts. Charlotte Brontë, aged nineteen, looks back with a poignant sense of loss to the shared childhood visions upon which the commonplace reality of working for a living has impinged. This theme divides itself into four curious symbols — web, water, seed and branch. There is a sense of a double perspective of time: first, early childhood, during which the dream the Brontë children created in terms of these symbols appeared the only reality; secondly, young adulthood, in which empirical reality in the form of 'darkly shaded life' appears to eclipse the validity of the dream. But, Charlotte Brontë asserts, in some strange corner of the mind the four images which correspond to their vision have been developing and expanding throughout the period when the Brontës were themselves growing up. It is probably no accident that there are four main symbols for the four children (including of course Branwell), nor that the symbolism itself with the passage of time has taken on an oddly surreal quality. The web, for instance, is now light-giving.

> Faded! the web is still of air,
>   But how its folds are spread,
> And from its tints of crimson clear
>   How deep a glow is shed.
> The light of an Italian sky
> Where clouds of sunset lingering lie
>   Is not more ruby-red.

It does not reflect light generated by a source in the empirical world outside the mind: rather, it emits from its own nature a crimson light and simultaneously has expanded beyond itself. Each image in turn is now developed by the poet until it becomes extreme, almost

13

absurd. The infinitesimal becomes giant, cosmic, as for instance the original spring which has grown into an ocean 'where armèd fleets may ride', a strange detail evoking the warrior spirits of the Angrian legend and emphasizing the pictorial quality of Charlotte's imagination when moral and rational considerations were not inhibiting it. What has happened is that the tiny seed of fantasy planted in childhood has become a fruitful and sustaining myth, which the adult human being can call upon at will. This is one of the solutions Charlotte Brontë found for her desperate sense of loneliness and deprivation within society.

The trouble was that she did not really believe it. What strikes one about 'We wove a web' is the way that after an impressive introduction (comparable perhaps with the surreal beauty of Emily's 'The Philosopher's Conclusion') dealing with the nature of fantasy, the momentum is lost as the author gives an instance of the vision she has analysed, in jogging rhythm and pedestrian rhyme, which turns out to be nothing more than an heroic set-piece whose only claim to epic status could be its intolerable length. Poetically, the dream does not measure up to the intensity of the need to dream, and this indicates a certain lack of conviction as to the capacity of the Angrian (or indeed any) fantasy to stand as a viable alternative to the real world. It is always in practice rather a resort into which one flees than a spiritual resource to be drawn on and nourished by.

This failure to establish herself in either the real or the imaginary worlds may account for the depression which broods over most of Charlotte Brontë's adult poems. In ''Tis not the air I wished to play', a swift melodic form is at variance with its theme — that depression without the possibility of heroic action which makes life appear simply an extended period of waiting for some event which is more or less certain never to occur. The world is just a place of insomnia and boredom, where even 'wild distress' would be desirable because it would allow positive connection with the world through activity. There is a sense of life's continuum as going in very slow motion, and yet it passes relentlessly too before one can catch hold of it. The central statement is 'Life will be gone ere I have lived'. Characteristic of the mood of Anne as much as of Charlotte, this is a fretful admission not only of failure to discover the kind of role available to most members of society, but also inability to create a tenable alternative. Just as her heroines, Jane Eyre, Caroline Helstone and Lucy Snowe, are excluded from opportunity to marry or to find truly satisfying work, so Charlotte Brontë feels herself unfairly disqualified from the excitements due to the young.

The solution in this, and in most, cases, is not the Angrian remedy, but a philosophy of stoicism. Charlotte's typical reaction to her predicament is a confrontation of her own image in the mirror which is the poem, and then a bitter renunciation of happiness in favour of 'Reason'. Reason dictates that what we cannot avoid we must accept, making no outrageous demands on the world: 'she' is the friend of 'Patience' and the way to God. But Charlotte Brontë is not particularly taken with her. In *Villette*, Lucy Snowe says,

> This hag, this Reason, would not let me look up, or smile, or hope; she could not rest until I were altogether crushed, cowed, broken in, and broken down. According to her, I was born only to work for a piece of bread, to await the pains of death, and steadily through all life to despond.

The relationship between Charlotte Brontë and Reason in the poems is never other than a coerced one. If circumstances were different, they would divorce and never communicate again. But as things are, she unwillingly embraces Reason and the affiliated virtues in poems such as "Tis not the air' and the 1845 poem explicitly entitled 'Reason', written, along with the poem of 1847, 'He saw my heart's woe', in anguished response to M. Heger's embarrassed and silent rejection of her.

'Reason' acknowledges candidly her motive for resorting to the rational way of life: her lack of beauty induces aspirations, 'Reason — Science — Learning — Thought', which for her come second to the great aim of affection. It is no wonder her friend Harriet Martineau, the famous campaigner for political economy, mesmerism and assorted causes, above all feminism, was so disgusted by Charlotte Brontë's glorification of passion, as though there were no other worthy aspiration in life for women. If Charlotte Brontë was a feminist (and she made brave statements for liberty and equality) she was one not on instinct but through pressure of circumstance. She was trapped into desire for liberty. A poem like 'Reason' makes this very clear. There is never any question that the life of the mind is the less attractive option, which cannot subdue the urges of the heart or recompense their frustration. Charlotte Brontë is faithful to Reason only 'because most desolate', never doubting that man falls back on rationality without loving it. And yet conversely she is aware that an insistence on facing the reasoned truth and subjugating oneself to it gives one a moral stature above that which is possible to the lucky and the beautiful. However, the feeling of 'Reason' becomes more bitter in the following poem, 'He saw my heart's woe'. There are two heroes in this poem, each the complement of the other. The first is her sexual idol, represented in terms of unconsciously phallic imagery as 'stirless as a tower', whose power is menacing in its indifference, and to whom her own reaction is a violent one. She is a fugitive from the first to the second hero, the Christian God who carries the other, opposite attribute of the male, fatherly tenderness. The urge to be protected and to worship what protects is a motif which runs throughout Charlotte Brontë's work.

And yet the sorrowful state I have described is not by any means the sole preoccupation of her poetry, and it is in order to emphasize this that I have included in the selection so many of her early verses, written in her teens. There are frankly foolish jingles like those beginning 'Oh, thou great, thou mighty tower' and 'Of College I am tired', the latter a jaunty poem spoken by her favourite imaginary hero, Lord Charles Wellesley, who apparently keeps a menagerie consisting of such rarities as rejoicing apes and a parrot with a 'lovely voice'. It is refreshing to realize that Charlotte possessed a sense of humour at this period of her life (thirteen to fourteen) and sad to reflect how easily it was mislaid. It is also a great encouragement to read a poem like 'Gods of the Old Mythology' which reveals what an unladylike person she must have been in young adulthood when she wrote this burlesque, full of invective, spurious erudition and the consciousness of being magnificently absurd.

16

In 1850, after Emily Brontë's death, Charlotte wrote of her that 'Stronger than a man, simpler than a child, her nature stood alone.' This tribute does more than crystallize Emily's essential qualities in a very moving way: it allows a double perspective on them. For Charlotte meant that nothing on earth could stand comparison with her sister's character, and equally that the power and simplicity which constituted the beauty of that character made her not simply unique, but consciously unique.

Emily Brontë would have nothing to do with society, loathed strangers and withdrew into silence and surliness if unfamiliar people invaded her territory. She wrote poems about solitude, and published the most violent, amoral novel of the nineteenth century, which gave the majority of its reviewers palpitations and would no doubt have made her a social outcast had she ever been within society long enough to be cast out of it. Loving the moors and her home, she was incapable of spiritual survival away from Yorkshire; perhaps it is this tendency, at once a childish refusal to abandon security and a powerful, independent rejection of worldly values, that reveals most clearly the qualities Charlotte Brontë notices in her.

Such a rejection involved less a withdrawal from reality than a dedication of herself to another, inner kind of experience. For this reason, an understanding of Emily Brontë as a poet depends far more on a grasp of the fantasy world she shared with Anne than on details of autobiography, for many of her finest poems were written as part of the Gondal saga, whose narrative framework has now been lost but whose main themes can be inferred from the poems and diary papers she and Anne left. To give an indication of the main outlines of this turbulent imaginary world is also to define the nature and preoccupations of Emily Brontë's mind.

In the land of Gondal, all qualities are absolute and immortal, all beings finite and mortal. It is a universe of polarities, in which both the gentle and the violent are heroes, carrying their emotions to extremes which to the protagonists themselves appear to represent the very proof of their existence. If they ceased to love absolutely or hate absolutely, they would cease to be. There is constant warfare between armies or individuals, and there is incessant mutiny within the individual himself against the conditions of his existence. Will is the dominating force in the Gondal drama: it is exerted by one soul against another and issues in the subjection of the victim, either in imprisonment (in 'Julian M. and A. G. Rochelle'), in eternal isolation from a loved object (the 'Song' beginning 'O between distress and pleasure') or in his death ('Death that struck when I was most confiding').

But another kind of will also stalks Gondal's people and seems to prey upon them: strange destinies loiter just out of sight and sardonically direct operations. The material world lies around like a corrosive element ready to pollute the creature who is willing to abandon the integrity of his solitude or passion to touch it. It appears as a kind of blight imposed by an inhumane God whose attributes include the capacity to inflict lifelong punishment for error as in 'This summer wind, with thee and me', and the eviction of man from grace, even after death:

> Compassion reigns a little while,
> Revenge eternally.

While there is also the possibility of unlimited divine mercy, many of Gondal's sinners like the protagonist of 'Shed no tears o'er that tomb' seem to be the property of an intransigent God.

Because of this, lost spirits in plenty wander the universe of Gondal, and in poem after poem one comes upon the figure of the moral reject, at once perpetrator and victim of his own exile. Neither the nature of his transgression nor the attitude to be adopted towards it is precisely defined. The child loved by Augusta Almeda in 'Sleep not, dream not' is, it appears, subject to 'relentless laws' that make real virtue and joy inaccessible on earth. She predicts his inevitable perversion as a result of his encounter with the condition to which he is doomed. The child, born with angelic innocence, will sweep through the entire spectrum of moral possibilities in order to become his own opposite. But the nature of opposites is such that they must always be attributes of an identical kind of phenomenon. The good and evil, enticing and repellent, aspects of the Gondal universe, are strangely intimate with one another. In this poem the doomed child is described as an 'enthusiast'. Extremist and zealot, he is at the beginning of life an enthusiast for holiness, at the end for unholiness, but this only seems to add to his magic for the narrator.

18

This moral ambiguity is central to Emily Brontë's work, both in her poetry and in *Wuthering Heights*. It is as glamorous to be 'hell-like in heart and misery', to be fallen and lost in the spiritually melodramatic world of Gondal, as to be an innocent. The intrusive stranger in 'And now the house-dog', prefiguring Heathcliff, cuts a sinister path into the homely dwelling of the shepherd and his family. The domestic world is menaced and disturbed by a visitation from an unknown dimension beyond its imagination, as the stranger, dark and chillingly free of the decencies of family life, exerts an extraordinary allure on the very people who resist that alien experience. There is both Byronism and satanism in the Gondal hero, but he is more of a symbolic figure, representing an intrusion from the unconscious region of experience into the common-sense light of day. Dark in complexion and inexplicable in motivation, he carries a mixture of the attraction and terror commonly attached to those elements of the human psyche which are too amoral, instinctual and unintelligible to reason to be accepted happily by the individual secure in orthodox social patterns. Heathcliff is an archetype of the subconscious mind, just as the Gondal hero of 'And now the house-dog', in the 'nameless' quality in his face which fascinated by being indefinable; in the ambiguity of his presence; in the way Emily Brontë has to define him by negatives, by what he is *not*, derives from and embodies repressed human nature.

The Gondal hero, then, is an unregenerate spirit, representing a world in which reason has little validity. And nobody addicted to the logic of common sense will find much to interest him in Emily Brontë's poetry. Gondal had no border separating it from the fabric of her real self, and although she kept two notebooks, one for Gondal, one for other poems, this does not mean that the creator of the Gondal myth lived a spiritual life different in kind to the myth itself. For what her imaginary characters are and assert corresponds closely with Emily's apparently more personal emotions in poems like 'Riches I hold in light esteem' or 'No coward soul is mine'. The Gondals are split off fragments of her own larger personality. In most authors, one or two central characters are patronized by their creator in a particular way: they are favourites, cherished by his subjectivity. In Emily Brontë's poetry, the fact that she does not

19

appear to identify herself specifically with any character stems from her identification with all, 'good' and 'bad'. It is an inclusive vision, in which the sum of persons and emotions equals the author's self. Consequently, her Gondal characters are perhaps less personalities than abstractions from personality, 'spirits', whose struggles may be seen as corresponding to those disparate elements in herself of which she speaks in 'The Philosopher's Conclusion' as at war within her spirit, and all of which, significantly, 'Heaven could not hold'. The timeless elegy beginning 'Cold in the earth', addressed by Rosina Alcona to Julius Brenzaida, is uttered by a woman who has been unfaithful to a succession of lovers and husbands, to a dead husband whose past was a web of tyrannies, conquests and treachery. This ability of Emily Brontë's to sympathize with the more apparently deplorable aspects of human nature should warn one against the sentimentalizing attitude to her which sometimes prevails.

Indeed, it would not be an exaggeration to say that Emily Brontë is one of the great egoists of our literature. Her theme is liberty, and a liberty conceived less as the overflow of love than as a function of solitude. Her stance is constantly one of withdrawal from her kind, as though freedom were only tenable when you had fended off the claims that encroached on the spirit from fellow creatures. At the summit of life was visionary experience: at its lowest point correspondence with the human herd engrossed in inane, unworthy concerns. Always she is at pains to distinguish herself from the orthodoxies practised by the human rubbish which she assumes populates the world outside. In 'There was a time', she speaks of her disgust with man's truthlessness and of her own proud superiority to this; in 'No coward soul is mine', she remarks casually that all the faiths and ideologies that have preoccupied the human mind are without exception spurious by comparison with her own belief, whose source is herself:

> Vain are the thousand creeds
> That move men's hearts, unutterably vain . . .

This is the most invincible conceit. It betrays a *hubris* shocking in its inhumanity, and yet in the terms in which it expresses itself in her poetry, this pride rather excites than disgusts, and seems to develop into a kind of self-transcending egoism because, like Wordsworth's, it produces a vision which is truly philosophical. For rejection of a material world with all its implications is the essential preliminary to mystical experience, and this will also involve obliteration of her own personality, so as to become, as she explains in 'I'm happiest when most away',

only spirit wandering wide
Through infinite immensity.

She wrote this poem at the age of nineteen, when already she was trying to find language capable of suggesting the nature of the soul's adventure in escaping time and space and the sentient, selfconscious human framework. A flood of poetry written approximately between the ages of twenty-four and twenty-six celebrates the same pursuit of liberty, understood as an entire rejection of corporeality in poems like 'Aye, there it is!'; as union with the natural world in 'Shall Earth no more inspire thee'; as rejection of reason in favour of the imagination in 'To Imagination' and 'O thy bright eyes must answer now', and as a kind of annunciation in the Gondal poem known as 'The Prisoner'.

Associated with the idea of the spirit's frustration at its immersion in the body is often the imagery of imprisonment, and connected with its leap into liberty through visionary experience one encounters recurrent and haunting imagery of stars. In 'How Clear She Shines', Emily Brontë imagines herself lying at night looking out of the sublunary world into the quiet of the universe beyond, where she hopes that the clustered stars are innocent of the squalor that characterizes earth. Juxtaposed with scathing condemnation of our condition in the world, the stars indicate a possible state of being, accessible to man's contemplation but not germane to the world in which he finds himself. Perhaps the most luminous account of visionary experience is embedded in the Gondal poem written in 1845 when she was twenty-seven and had only two years left to live and a handful of poems still to write. This is 'The Prisoner'. I have excluded the bulk of the poem, for description of girls in dungeons is an all too familiar feature of Gondal and Angrian society. But the convention of the imprisoned girl, victimized and defiant, deepens here: she is a metaphor for the idea that the liberty which eludes humanity at its apparently most free is available paradoxically to one who is, to all intents and purposes, deprived of it. The process of liberation, beginning as a kind of visitation, is personalized (as in many of Emily Brontë's accounts of the experience) as a conjunction of two spirits, in an effort to give an impression of the rapture of the experience.

> He comes with western winds, with evening's wandering airs,
> With that clear dusk of heaven that brings the thickest stars;
> Winds take a pensive tone, and stars a tender fire,
> And visions rise and change which kill me with desire.

Peace through the conspiracy of all these kinds of beauty preludes the soaring of the spirit off the earth and into the immensity of sky and stars. Yet at the crucial moment of liberation consciousness returns and there is the anticlimactic fall to earth in the inevitable failure of the living person to shed individual identity and sense perceptions. For the paradox reposing at the centre of her wish to be free was that only death could fulfil it, but that, once dead, you are beyond fulfilment. Possibly this explains why Emily met her own death in such a way that Charlotte could speak of her 'turning her dying eyes reluctantly from the pleasant sun'.

Anne Brontë

The greatest predator on the Brontë family was not consumption but Calvinism. Its ugly face is seen peering over the shoulder of Charlotte in her earlier years and of Anne throughout her life, insinuating to them that they are, through some barbarous freak of predestination, not amongst the company of the saved. Charlotte, looking through Anne Brontë's papers after her death, was horrified to discover the despair that had occupied the soul of one she had thought so secure in her faith. Reading Anne's religious poems is like watching a lifelong struggle between negative and positive elements for possession of her spirit: there is something of Cowper in it, something too of Faustus, though this battle provides the satisfaction of knowing that faith has won, just about, as Anne goes to her death.

Calvinism with its God of damnation who has elected the few to be saved, the many to be disposed of in fire and brimstone, partly had Anne Brontë for its victim, partly was itself her victim. On the one hand, as so many of her poems show, she was subject to its threat that certain persons have already been excluded from Heaven, and felt, through a deep conviction of her own sinfulness, that she was going to turn out to be one of these spiritual derelicts. On the other hand, she was herself too loving a person not to loathe the very idea of such a God, who with no sense of decency arbitrarily damned the creatures he had chosen to make and sworn to love. She reacted then with fury against the Calvinists, and this response finds expression in a beautiful, angry poem of 1843 called 'A Word to the "Elect"'. Calvinism either correctly assumed a vicious God with whom it would be morally unworthy to collaborate, or else Calvinism was false. The first idea being intolerable, she chose the second, and one finds even in her most pessimistic poems a current which resists despair and strives toward repose in the love of a tolerant God.

Yet she went even further than this in her resistance to contemporary orthodoxies. Not everyone believed in the Calvinist God's random decision to damn or save the individual soul, but almost all nineteenth-century Christian sects accepted a God who pitched the unrepentant into hell after their death. This retributive God was also intolerable to Anne Brontë, for, even supposing him to be just, he was insensitive, and compassion seemed to her the highest value one could postulate. The degradation and slow death of Branwell reinforced her insistence on an all-merciful God. Anyone who has read Helen Huntingdon's outburst against the doctrine of damnation in Anne's novel, *The Tenant of Wildfell Hall*, will realize to what extent she was an individualist, forging her own criticism of conventions which she considered inadequate: of all three sisters, she was the most outspoken radical, not only on religious matters but also on social issues such as feminism, marriage, education and personal liberty.

And yet there is something in Anne Brontë of the gentle being Charlotte saw in her. This is reflected in the ingenuous, simple form of the poems. It emerges in the way in which the carnivorous nature of a religion of which she profoundly disapproves still terrorizes her. Calvinism leaves an image on her mind which she is able to counter but never quite to abolish. In poems like 'Despondency', 'To Cowper', 'A Prayer', and others written in her middle twenties, Anne Brontë wrestles against her despair of God's love, and the poem itself is an act of faith which, by asserting the reality of God's care, hopes to prove it to her own doubting mind. 'A Prayer' is a brief and poignant hymn which has been included in the Baptist Hymnal. One understands why: its tentative pursuit of meaning has a universal quality, and is moving by virtue of the emotional understatement Anne Brontë manages to achieve in those austere quatrains which characterize so many of her best poems. The effect is achieved by accumulating negatives to define her own spiritual position, building to the climactic statement of the positive she seeks, which is God. Her typical stance in these religious poems is a desperate humility before a Creator who is feared more than he is loved. Hers is essentially a passive role which seeks to be worked upon by a will which exists in terms of an energy outside herself. While Emily Brontë will create God out of her own personality, Anne cowers, but with dignity acknowledges her terror of a God whose nature is beyond hers.

The castaway image in 'A Prayer' is significant, recalling as it does the Cowper of 'The Castaway', to whose mild and tortured personality, repudiated by a murderously cold-hearted God, the poem dedicated to him proves her devotion. The final stanza of 'To Cowper' evokes and exploits the technique of 'The Castaway' by revealing at the last possible moment that the poem's apparent hero was not necessarily the real one. While Cowper's poem ends:

> No voice divine the storm allay'd,
> No light propitious shone;
> When, snatch'd from all effectual aid,
> We perish'd, each alone:
> But I beneath a rougher sea,
> And whelm'd in deeper gulphs than he.

Anne Brontë concludes:

> Yet, should thy darkest fears be true,
> If Heaven be so severe,
> That such a soul as thine is lost, —
> Oh! how shall I appear?

Cowper contends that his situation is more terrible than that of the drowned man he has described; Anne Brontë holds that, if this is true, then hers is worse again. She may scorn the Calvinist God for his brutalities but that figure has fatally seized on her imagination and wrings from her the haunting admission of her own frailty summed up in 'A Prayer' in the recognition,

> I cannot say my faith is strong,
> I dare not hope my love is great

with its consequent yearning that God will 'take the heart I cannot give'. She perceives herself through negatives, as though not entirely convinced of her own reality, by contrast to Emily who sees herself as the central positive in a negative universe.

Liberty, understood in the context of Anne Brontë's religious vision, cannot be interpreted in quite the same way as in her sister's poetry. Anne's religious poems define it as a state to be achieved through discipline and not through abandon, as a glance at a poem of 1841, 'Despondency', will confirm. Chains anchor the soul to its own torpidity: it is not to be trusted. Emancipation from this painful state would not be into individual freedom but into specifically Christian self-control. And yet there is much in Anne's poetry linking it to Emily's, and most particularly in the Gondal poems. Numerous incarcerated ladies, for instance, like Marina Sabia in 'A Voice from the Dungeon' and Alexandrina Zenobia in 'The North Wind', utter complaints. Here, as in many of the Brontës' poems, 'liberty' is a key rhyming word, and in this context, Emily and Anne would mean the same thing by it. But the inhabitant of Gondal seems to have been slightly domesticated by Anne: husband and children are as desirable as visions of liberty to her imprisoned heroines.

However, the myth of the fall which informs the Gondal story was as germane to Anne's conception of things as to Emily's. The Gondal myth implicitly concerns humanity's separation into distinctive units, individuals, each searching back for his source. In the figure of the child, Anne and Emily recreate that early union, but for Anne it may be achieved through having as much as through being one. Her 'Verses to a Child' (1838), 'Past Days' (1843) and 'Dreams' (1845) show her reaching back, in her own person and that of a Gondal character, out of the life which work or misfortune has drained of significance. Gondal and reality meet here in the symbolic figure of the child, and in a sense each of these poems is a lament for the achievement of adulthood. None of the Brontës was particularly pleased to find herself grown up. In 'Past Days', childhood is remembered as a period when everything flowed together in effortless reciprocity of friendship and enjoyment, when the individual had not yet been parted from the context to which he belonged, splintered off into consciousness, but was an organic part of the whole. In that larger unity even the experience of grief is a response to an emotion intuited in another.

The idea of a lost Paradise, then, is an example of the considerable common ground in Anne's and Emily's poetry which is recognizable not only in shared themes but also by phrases which echo each other in poems written more or less simultaneously. The Gondal elegies often reveal similarities which can only be the consequence of the growth of what one might think of as a mutual mind. Anne Brontë's 'Night' and Emily's 'R. Alcona to J. Brenzaida', each written early in

26

1845, turn on a crucial, nearly identical idea and phrase, 'Cold in the grave', 'Cold in the earth', which appears to originate with Anne and to be developed dramatically by Emily. Other poems in the selection too could equally well have been written by either sister, for they seem to mingle Anne's delicate moral sense with Emily's apprehension of a world of struggling polarities. These include the two 'Songs', which, composed on two consecutive days in September 1845, deal with civil war in Gondal and are written as an excited, probing analysis of the idea of liberty. The situation in Gondal which seems to have obtained at the time of writing had presumably developed out of that elucidated in Anne's diary paper of 31 July of that year: 'The Gondals are at present in a sad state. The Republicans are uppermost, but the Royalists are not quite overcome.' By September, on the evidence of the 'Songs', the Republicans must have routed their enemies and got the nation under their heels. They sing here, in these grim but melodious lyrics, of the anticlimax of achievement, the heroism of defeat. They who are the predators where they used to be the prey find that there is something more fulfilling about constand retreat than in being the marauder. The Republicans in the poem, having been released from the oppression of being hunted round the hills, 'can' do what they like, such as ravening round the hills in their turn after their defeated enemies, but there is a nastiness to the taste of such liberty. In the third verse, the hare is a beautiful image of innocence in the face of oppression: terrified and startled at every moment, leading an existence without choice, he is yet seen as having a moral justification not available to the victor. With remarkable intellectual control, Anne Brontë manages in these poems to create an ambiguity on the verbs 'can' and 'must', which may fruitfully be related to the ethos of many poems in the Gondal saga. Those who 'must', the defeated, exiled and divided, have a life-giving vision of liberty which is unique to them. Those who 'can', the lucky and the tyrannous, may also be driven along by a law which victimizes them in forcing them to be aggressors. The hunted creature in the second 'Song', having nothing between him and the sky, is at liberty. It is almost as if, in the world of Gondal and Anne's and Emily's imagination, the desire for liberty was much more significant than its actual achievement: as though this might

27

even prove a positive disaster, rebellion being more interesting than contentment.

Had all the prisoners in the Brontë world been emancipated, the unregenerate redeemed, the ugly made beautiful, the exiles rehabilitated, who can doubt that they would have drearily repeated with Anne's Republican,

> Is *this* the end we struggled to obtain?
> Oh, for the wandering Outlaw's life again!

POEMS BY CHARLOTTE BRONTË

Lines Addressed to 'The Tower of All Nations'

Oh, thou great, thou mighty tower!
   Rising up so solemnly
O'er all this splendid, glorious city:
   This city of the sea;

Thou seem'st, as silently I gaze,
   Like a pillar of the sky:
So lofty is thy structure grey;
   So massive, and so high!

The dome of Heaven is o'er thee hung
   With its maze of silver stars;
The earth is round about thee spread
   With its eternal bars.

And such a charming doggerel
   As this was never wrote,
Not even by the mighty
   And high Sir Walter Scott!

*Written upon the Occasion of the Dinner Given to the Literati of
the Glasstown, which was attended by all the Great Men of the
present time: Soldier, Sailor, Poet and Painter, Architect, Politician,
Novelist and Romancer.*

The splendid Hall is blazing with many a glowing light,
And a spirit-like effulgence mild, a flood of glory bright,
Flows round the stately pillars, nor dimly dies away
In the arched roof of solid stone, but there each golden ray
Shines with a brightened splendour, a radiance rich and fair,
And then falls amid the palace vast, and lightens up the air,
Till the atmosphere around is one continuous flow
Of streaming lustre, brilliant light, and liquid topaz glow.
All beneath this gorgeousness there sits a chosen band

Of genius high and courage bold: the noblest of the land.
The feast is spread, and brightly the purple juice doth shine
In the yellow gold magnificent: the sparkling generous wine!
And all between the thunders of patriotic cheers
Is heard the sounding orchestra, while the inspiring tears
Of a rich southern vineyard are quaffed to wish the health
Of some most noble warrior fierce, a nation's power and wealth.
And then arises slowly an orator of might
And pours a flood of eloquence upon this festal night.
The gentle stream flows dimpling 'mong rhetoric's bright flowers,
Poises in wild sublimity on eagle's wing-high towers;
And lost amid the cloudy curtains of his might,
Far beyond the common ken his spirit has taken flight.
For awhile he dwells in glory within the solemn veil,
Then returns upon the smoother seas of beauty fair to sail.
The scene this night is joyous within these palace walls,
But ere ten passing centuries are gone these lofty halls
May stand in darksome ruin: these stately pillars high
May echo back far other sounds than those which sweetly fly
Among their light bold arches, and mingling softly rise
In a wild enchanting melody, which tremulously dies;
The yell of the hyena, the bloody-tiger's howl,
May be heard in this magnificence, mixed with the lion's growl;
While in the cold pale moonlight may stand the ruins grey,
These marble columns mouldering, and gladness fled away!

Home-Sickness

Of College I am tired; I wish to be at home,
Far from the pompous tutor's voice, and the hated school-boy's
                                                        groan.

I wish that I had freedom to walk about at will;
That I no more was troubled by my Greek and slate and quill.

I wish to see my kitten, to hear my ape rejoice,
To listen to my nightingale's or parrot's lovely voice.

And England does not suit me: it's cold and full of snow;
So different from black Africa's warm, sunny, genial glow.

I'm shivering in the day-time, and shivering all the night:
I'm called poor, startled, withered wretch, and miserable wight!

And oh! I miss my brother, I miss his gentle smile
Which used so many long dark hours of sorrow to beguile.

I miss my dearest mother; I now no longer find
Aught half so mild as she was, — so careful and so kind.

Oh, I have not my father's, my noble father's arms
To guard me from all wickedness, and keep me safe from harms.

I hear his voice no longer; I see no more his eye
Smile on me in my misery: to whom now shall I fly?

from *Retrospection*

We wove a web in childhood,
    A web of sunny air;
We dug a spring in infancy
    Of water pure and fair;

We sowed in youth a mustard seed,
    We cut an almond rod;
We are now grown up to riper age —
    Are they withered in the sod?

Are they blighted, failed and faded,
    Are they mouldered back to clay?
For life is darkly shaded;
    And its joys fleet fast away.

Faded! the web is still of air,
    But how its folds are spread,

And from its tints of crimson clear
   How deep a glow is shed.
The light of an Italian sky
Where clouds of sunset lingering lie
   Is not more ruby-red.

But the spring was under a mossy stone,
   Its jet may gush no more.
Hark! sceptic bid thy doubts be gone,
   Is that a feeble roar
Rushing around thee? Lo! the tide
Of waves where armèd fleets may ride
Sinking and swelling, frowns and smiles
An ocean with a thousand isles
   And scarce a glimpse of shore.

The mustard-seed in distant land
   Bends down a mighty tree,
The dry unbudding almond-wand
   Has touched eternity.
There came a second miracle
Such as on Aaron's sceptre fell,
And sapless grew like life from heath,
Bud, bloom and fruit in mingling wreath
All twined the shrivelled off-shoot round
As flowers lie on the lone grave-mound.

Dream that stole o'er us in the time
When life was in its vernal clime,
Dream that still faster o'er us steals
   As the mild star of spring declining
The advent of that day reveals,
   That glows on Sirius' fiery shining:
Oh! as thou swellest, and as the scenes
   Cover this cold world's darkest features,
Stronger each change my spirit weans
   To bow before thy god-like creatures.

The Wounded Stag

Passing amid the deepest shade
    Of the wood's sombre heart,
Last night I saw a wounded deer
    Laid lonely and apart.

Such light as pierced the crowded boughs
    (Light scattered, scant, and dim),
Passed through the fern that formed his couch,
    And centred full on him.

Pain trembled in his weary limbs,
    Pain filled his patient eye;
Pain-crushed amid the shadowy fern
    His branchy crown did lie.

Where were his comrades? where his mate?
    All from his death-bed gone!
And he, thus struck and desolate,
    Suffered and bled alone.

Did he feel what a man might feel,
    Friend-left and sore distrest?
Did Pain's keen dart, and Grief's sharp sting
    Strive in his mangled breast?

Did longing for affection lost
    Barb every deadly dart;
Love unrepaid, and Faith betrayed, —
    Did these torment his heart?

No! leave to man his proper doom!
    These are the pangs that rise
Around the bed of state and gloom,
    Where Adam's offspring dies!

'Turn not now for comfort here'

Turn not now for comfort here;
    The lamps are quenched, the moors are gone;
Cold and lonely, dim and drear,
    Void are now those hills of stone.

Sadly sighing, Anvale woods
    Whisper peace to my decay;
Fir-tree over pine-tree broods
    Dark and high and piled away.

Gone are all who saw my glory
    Fill on festal nights the trees
Distant lit, now silver hoary,
    Bowed they to the freshening breeze.

They are dead who heard at night
    Woods and winds and waters sound,
Where my casements cast their light
    Red upon the snow-piled ground.

Some from afar in foreign regions,
    Some from drear suffering — wild unrest,
All light on land and winged legions
    Fill the old woods and parent nest.

'He could not sleep! — the couch of war'

He could not sleep! — the couch of war,
    Simple and rough beneath him spread,
Scared sleep away, and scattered far
    The balm its influence might have shed.

He could not sleep! his temples, pressed
    To the hard pillow, throbbed with pain;

The belt around his noble breast
　　His heart's wild pulse could scarce restrain.

And stretched in feverish unrest
　　Awake the great commander lay;
In vain the cooling night-wind kissed
　　His brow with its reviving play,

As through the open window streaming
　　All the fresh scents of night it shed,
And mingled with the moonlight, beaming
　　In broad clear lustre round his bed.

Out in the night Cirhala's water
　　Lifted its voice of swollen floods;
On its wild shores the bands of slaughter
　　Lay camped amid its savage woods.

Beneath the lonely Auberge's shelter
　　The Duke's rough couch that night was spread;
The sods of battle round him welter
　　In noble blood that morning shed;

And, gorged with prey, and now declining
　　From all the fire of glory won,
Watchful and fierce he lies repining
　　O'er what may never be undone.

The Teacher's Monologue

The room is quiet, thoughts alone
　　People its mute tranquillity;
The yoke put off, the long task done, —
　　I am, as it is bliss to be,
Still and untroubled. Now, I see,
　　For the first time, how soft the day

37

O'er waveless water, stirless tree,
  Silent and sunny, wings its way.
Now, as I watch that distant hill,
  So faint, so blue, so far removed,
Sweet dreams of home my heart may fill,
  That home where I am known and loved:
It lies beyond; yon azure brow
  Parts me from all Earth holds for me;
And, morn and eve, my yearnings flow
  Thitherward tending, changelessly.
My happiest hours, ay! all the time,
  I love to keep in memory,
Lapsed among moors, ere life's first prime
  Decayed to dark anxiety.

Sometimes, I think a narrow heart
  Makes me thus mourn those far away,
And keeps my love so far apart
  From friends and friendships of to-day;
Sometimes, I think 'tis but a dream
  I treasure up so jealously,
All the sweet thoughts I live on seem
  To vanish into vacancy:
And then, this strange, coarse world around
  Seems all that's palpable and true;
And every sight and every sound
  Combines my spirit to subdue
To aching grief; so void and lone
  Is Life and Earth — so worse than vain,
The hopes that, in my own heart sown,
  And cherished by such sun and rain
As Joy and transient Sorrow shed,
  Have ripened to a harvest there:
Alas! methinks I hear it said,
  'Thy golden sheaves are empty air.'
All fades away; my very home
  I think will soon be desolate;

38

I hear, at times, a warning come
    Of bitter partings at its gate;
And, if I should return and see
    The hearth-fire quenched, the vacant chair;
And hear it whispered mournfully,
    That farewells have been spoken there,
What shall I do, and whither turn?
Where look for peace? When cease to mourn?
        *   *   *

'Tis not the air I wished to play,
    The strain I wished to sing;
My wilful spirit slipped away
    And struck another string.
I neither wanted smile nor tear,
    Bright joy nor bitter woe,
But just a song that sweet and clear,
    Though haply sad, might flow.

A quiet song, to solace me
    When sleep refused to come;
A strain to chase despondency
    When sorrowful for home.
In vain I try; I cannot sing;
    All feels so cold and dead
No wild distress, no gushing spring
    Of tears in anguish shed;

But all the impatient gloom of one
    Who waits a distant day,
When, some great task of suffering done,
    Repose shall toil repay.
For youth departs, and pleasure flies,
    And life consumes away,
And youth's rejoicing ardour dies
    Beneath this drear delay;

And Patience, weary with her yoke,
    Is yielding to despair,

And Health's elastic spring is broke
  Beneath the strain of care.
Life will be gone ere I have lived;
  Where now is Life's first prime?
I've worked and studied, longed and grieved,
  Through all that rosy time.

To toil, to think, to long, to grieve, —
  Is such my future fate?
The morn was dreary, must the eve
  Be also desolate?
Well, such a life at least makes Death
  A welcome, wished-for friend;
Then, aid me, Reason, Patience, Faith,
  To suffer to the end!

Diving

Look into thought and say what dost thou see;
  Dive, be not fearful how dark the waves flow;
Sing through the surge, and bring pearls up to me;
  Deeper, ay, deeper; the fairest lie low.

'I have dived, I have sought them, but none have I found;
  In the gloom that closed o'er me no form floated by;
As I sank through the void depths, so black and profound,
  How dim died the sun and how far hung the sky!

'What had I given to hear the soft sweep
  Of a breeze bearing life through that vast realm of death!
Thoughts were untroubled and dreams were asleep:
  The spirit lay dreadless and hopeless beneath.'

40

Gods of the Old Mythology

Gods of the old mythology, arise in gloom and storm;
Adramalec, bow down thy head; Nergal, dark fiend, thy form; —
The giant sons of Anakim bowed lowest at thy shrine,
And thy temple rose in Argob, with its hallowed groves of vine;
And there was eastern incense burnt, and there were garments
spread,
With the fine gold decked and broidered, and tinged with radiant
red, —
With the radiant red of furnace-flames that through the shadow
shone,
As the full moon, when on Sinai's top, her rising light is thrown.
Baal of Chaldaea, dread god of the sun,
Come from the towers of thy proud Babylon,
From the groves where the green palms of Media grow,
Where flowers of Assyria all fragrantly blow;
Where the waves of Euphrates glide deep as the sea
Washing the gnarled roots of Lebanon's tree.
Ashtaroth, curse of the Ammonites, rise
Decked with the beauty and light of the skies,
Let stars be thy crown and let mists round thee curl
Light as the gossamer, pure as the pearl.
Semele, soft vision, come glowing and brightly,
Come in a shell, like the Greek Aphrodite,
Come in the billowy rush of the foam,
From thy gold house in Elysium, roam
Where the bright purple blooms of glory
Picture forth thy goddess-story.
Come from thy blood-lit furnaces, most terrible and dread —
From thy most black and bloody flames, god Moloch, lift thy head,
Where the wild wail of infant lungs shrieks horribly alone,
And the fearful yelping of their tongues sounds like a demon's
groan.
There, their heart-riven mothers haste with burdened arms
raised up,
And offer in their agony to thee thy gory cup.

41

O Dagon! from thy threshold roll on thy fishy train
And fall upon thy face and hands and break thy neck again:
Enormous wretch, most beastly fiend, plague of the Philistine!
O'er the locked Ark I bid thee come with its Cherubim divine.
And Belial loathsome, where art thou? Dost hear my rampant
voice?
I mean to be obeyed, man, when I make such a noise.
My harp is screeching, ringing out, with a wild fevered moan,
And my lyre, like a sparrow with a sore throat, has a most
unearthly tone.
A bottle of brandy is in me, and my spirit is up on high,
And I'll make every man amongst ye pay the piper ere I die;
And as for thee, thou scoundrel, thou brimstone sulphurous
Mammon,
Let's have no more of thee nor of thy villainous gammon.
I'll be with you with a salt-whip most horrible for aye,
And I'll lash you till your hair turns as black as mine is grey.
You shall dwell in the red range while I blow the coals full fast,
And I'll make you feel the fury of a rushing furnace-blast,
Leap down the sweating rocks and the murderous caves of the pit,
And stamp with your hooves and lash with your tails and fire and
fury spit.
I'll be at you in a jiffy as fast as I can run,
But I'm riding now on the horns of the moon and the back of the
burning sun,
The wind is rushing before me and the clouds in a handgallop go,
And they are getting it properly when they fly a stiver too slow,
For the weed-slimy lands of the earth send up such a stink to me
That I'm fain to go on in my mad career, and soon shall I be
with ye.
I'm a noble fellow, flames I spew, I shall eat them up if I'm spared;
I'm going to the pit of sulphur blue, and my name is Thomas Aird.

Parting

There's no use in weeping,
 Though we are condemned to part;
There's such a thing as keeping
 A remembrance in one's heart:

There's such a thing as dwelling
 On the thought ourselves have nursed,
And with scorn and courage telling
 The world to do its worst.

We'll not let its follies grieve us,
 We'll just take them as they come;
And then every day will leave us
 A merry laugh for home.

When we've left each friend and brother,
 When we're parted, wide and far,
We will think of one another,
 As even better than we are.

Every glorious sight above us,
 Every pleasant sight beneath,
We'll connect with those that love us,
 Whom we truly love till death!

In the evening, when we're sitting
 By the fire, perchance alone,
Then shall heart with warm heart meeting,
 Give responsive tone for tone.

We can burst the bonds which chain us,
 Which cold human hands have wrought,
And where none shall dare restrain us
 We can meet again, in thought.

So there's no use in weeping,
   Bear a cheerful spirit still:
Never doubt that Fate is keeping
   Future good for present ill!

Preference

Not in scorn do I reprove thee,
   Not in pride thy vows I waive,
But, believe, I could not love thee,
   Wert thou prince and I a slave.
These, then, are thine oaths of passion?
   This, thy tenderness for me?
Judged, even, by thine own confession,
   Thou art steeped in perfidy.
Having vanquished, thou wouldst leave me!
   Thus I read thee long ago;
Therefore, dared I not deceive thee,
   Even with friendship's gentle show.
Therefore, with impassive coldness
   Have I never met thy gaze;
Though, full oft, with daring boldness,
   Thou thine eyes to mine didst raise.
Why that smile? Thou now art deeming
   This my coldness all untrue, —
But a mask of frozen seeming,
   Hiding secret fires from view.
Touch my hand, thou self-deceiver;
   Nay — be calm, for I am so:
Does it burn? Does my lip quiver?
   Has mine eye a troubled glow?
Canst thou call a moment's colour
   To my forehead — to my cheek?
Canst thou tinge their tranquil pallor
   With one flattering, feverish streak?
Am I marble? What! no woman

Could so calm before thee stand?
  Nothing living, sentient, human
Could so coldly take thy hand?
Yes — a sister might, a mother:
  My good-will is sisterly:
Dream not, then, I strive to smother
  Fires that inly burn for thee.
Rave not, rage not, wrath is fruitless,
  Fury cannot change my mind;
I but deem the feeling rootless
  Which so whirls in passion's wind.
Can I love? Oh, deeply — truly —
  Warmly — fondly — but not thee;
And my love is answered duly,
  With an equal energy.
Wouldst thou see thy rival? Hasten,
  Draw that curtain soft aside,
Look where yon thick branches chasten
  Noon, with shades of eventide.
In that glade, where foliage blending
  Forms a green arch overhead,
Sits thy rival, thoughtful bending
  O'er a stand with papers spread —
Motionless, his fingers plying
  That untired, unresting pen;
Time and tide unnoticed flying,
  There he sits — the first of men!
Man of conscience — man of reason;
  Stern, perchance, but ever just;
Foe to falsehood, wrong, and treason,
  Honour's shield, and virtue's trust!
Worker, thinker, firm defender
  Of Heaven's truth — man's liberty;
Soul of iron — proof to slander,
  Rock where founders tyranny.
Fame he seeks not — but full surely
  She will seek him, in his home;

This I know, and wait securely
    For the atoning hour to come.
To that man my faith is given,
    Therefore, soldier, cease to sue;
While God reigns in earth and Heaven,
    I to him will still be true!

Morning

Morning was in its freshness still,
    Noon yet far off with all its stir,
Cool early shade, calm leisure fill
    The silent hall and summer room.
Two hours I yet may number ere
Full glaring day brings tumult near
And lets intensive labour, care,
    Disturb my humble home.

Two hours! — how shall they speed with me,
    In measured task, toil self-assigned?
No, eager claim for liberty
    Some sense now urges in my mind
Through Fancy's realm of imagery
Some strange delight in ranging free;
Some joy that will not prisoned be,
    Brisk as the western wind.

It hurries back and brings the Past
    Sweetly before my soul;
It wings its way like rapid blast
    To the far Future's goal.
Pleasant the thoughts its pinions chase,
And bright though vague the dreamy place
Where tends its winged and ardent race
    Farther than Ocean's roll.

Each pleasant passage in my life
    I now live o'er again.
I pass the weary hours of strife,
    Forget the scenes of pain.
What scorn has said and Hate has done
Oblivion's veil lies dimly on,
And tears by Woe from Weakness won
    Remembrance cease to stain.

But every gift by Joy bestowed
    I count in numbers true;
And every hour that smoothly flowed
    This hour does well renew;
And if Love's whisper ever yet
My ear like note of music met,
This summer wind seems to repeat
    The tones with cadence due.

'Tis bitter sometimes to recall
    Illusions once deemed fair,
But in this golden moment all
    Doth fairy gilding wear;
And fond and fast the pulses beat
Departed Passion's shade to greet
Rising in transient vision sweet
    To colour empty air.

Master and Pupil

I gave, at first, attention close;
    Then interest warm ensued;
From interest, as improvement rose,
    Succeeded gratitude.

Obedience was no effort soon,
    And labour was no pain;

If tired, a word, a glance alone
    Would give me strength again.

From others of the studious band
    Ere long he singled me;
But only by more close demand
    And sterner urgency.

The task he from another took,
    From me he did reject;
He would no slight omission brook,
    And suffer no defect.

If my companions went astray,
    He scarce their wanderings blamed;
If I but faltered in the way,
    His anger fiercely flamed.

When sickness stayed awhile my course,
    He seemed impatient still,
Because his pupil's flagging force
    Could not obey his will.

One day when summoned to the bed
    Where pain and I did strive,
I heard him, as he bent his head,
    Say, 'God, she must revive!'

I felt his hand, with gentle stress,
    A moment laid on mine,
And wished to mark my consciousness
    By some responsive sign.

But powerless then to speak or move,
    I only felt, within,
The sense of Hope, the strength of Love,
    Their healing work begin.

And as he from the room withdrew,
　My heart his steps pursued;
I longed to prove, by efforts new,
　My speechless gratitude.

When once again I took my place,
　Long vacant, in the class,
Th'unfrequent smile across his face
　Did for one moment pass.

The lesson done; the signal made
　Of glad release and play,
He, as he passed, an instant stayed,
　One kindly word to say.

'Jane, till to-morrow you are free
　From tedious task and rule;
This afternoon I must not see
　That yet pale face in school.

'Seek in the garden-shades a seat,
　Far from the playground din;
The sun is warm, the air is sweet:
　Stay till I call you in.'

A long and pleasant afternoon
　I passed in those green bowers;
All silent, tranquil, and alone
　With birds, and bees, and flowers.

Yet, when my master's voice I heard
　Call, from the window, 'Jane!'
I entered, joyful, at the word,
　The busy house again.

He, in the hall, paced up and down;
　He paused as I passed by;

His forehead stern relaxed its frown;
    He raised his deep-set eye.

'Not quite so pale,' he murmured low.
    'Now, Jane, go rest awhile,'
And as I smiled his smoothened brow
    Returned as glad a smile.

My perfect health restored, he took
    His mien austere again;
And, as before, he would not brook
    The slightest fault from Jane.

The longest task, the hardest theme
    Fell to my share as erst,
And still I toiled to place my name
    In every study first.

He yet begrudged and stinted praise,
    But I had learnt to read
The secret meaning of his face,
    And that was my best meed.

Even when his hasty temper spoke
    In tones that sorrow stirred,
My grief was lulled as soon as woke
    By some relenting word.

And when he lent some precious book,
    Or gave some fragrant flower,
I did not quail to Envy's look,
    Upheld by Pleasure's power.

At last our school ranks took their ground,
    The hard-fought field I won;
The prize, a laurel-wreath, was bound
    My throbbing forehead on.

Low at my master's knee I bent,
    The offered crown to meet;
Its green leaves through my temples sent
    A thrill as wild as sweet.

The strong pulse of Ambition struck
    In every vein I owned;
At the same instant, bleeding broke
    A secret, inward wound.

The hour of triumph was to me
    The hour of sorrow sore;
A day hence I must cross the sea,
    Ne'er to recross it more.

An hour hence, in my master's room,
    I with him sat alone,
And told him what a dreary gloom
    O'er joy had parting thrown.

He little said; the time was brief,
    The ship was soon to sail;
And while I sobbed in bitter grief
    My master but looked pale.

They called in haste: he bade me go,
    Then snatched me back again;
He held me fast and murmured low,
    'Why will they part us, Jane?

'Were you not happy in my care?
    Did I not faithful prove?
Will others to my darling bear
    As true, as deep a love?

'O God, watch o'er my foster-child!
    Oh, guard her gentle head!

When winds are high and tempests wild
  Protection round her spread!

'They call again: leave then my breast;
  Quit thy true shelter, Jane;
But when deceived, repulsed, opprest,
  Come home to me again!'

Reason

Unloved I love, unwept I weep,
  Grief I restrain, hope I repress;
Vain is this anguish, fixed and deep,
  Vainer desires or means of bliss.

My life is cold, love's fire being dead;
  That fire self-kindled, self-consumed;
What living warmth erewhile it shed,
  Now to how drear extinction doomed!

Devoid of charm how could I dream
  My unasked love would e'er return?
What fate, what influence lit the flame
  I still feel inly, deeply burn?

Alas! there are those who should not love;
  I to this dreary band belong;
This knowing let me henceforth prove
  Too wise to list delusion's song.

No, Syren! Beauty is not mine;
  Affection's joy I ne'er shall know;
Lonely will be my life's decline,
  Even as my youth is lonely now.

Come Reason — Science — Learning — Thought —
  To you my heart I dedicate;

I have a faithful subject brought:
  Faithful because most desolate.

Fear not a wandering, feeble mind:
  Stern Sovereign, it is all your own
To crush, to cheer, to loose, to bind;
  Unclaimed, unshared, it seeks your throne.

Soft may the breeze of summer blow,
  Sweetly its sun in valleys shine;
All earth around with love may glow, —
  No warmth shall reach this heart of mine.

Vain boast and false! Even now the fire
  Though smothered, slacked, repelled, is burning
At my life's source; and stronger, higher,
  Waxes the spirit's trampled yearning.

It wakes but to be crushed again:
  Faint I will not, nor yield to sorrow;
Conflict and force will quell the brain;
  Doubt not I shall be strong to-morrow.

Have I not fled that I may conquer?
  Crost the dark sea in firmest faith
That I at last might plant my anchor
  Where love cannot prevail to death?

'He saw my heart's woe, discovered my soul's anguish'

He saw my heart's woe, discovered my soul's anguish,
  How in fever, in thirst, in atrophy it pined;
Knew he could heal, yet looked and let it languish, —
  To its moans spirit-deaf, to its pangs spirit-blind.

But once a year he heard a whisper low and dreary
  Appealing for aid, entreating some reply;

53

Only when sick, soul-worn, and torture-weary,
    Breathed I that prayer, heaved I that sigh.

He was mute as is the grave, he stood stirless as a tower;
    At last I looked up, and saw I prayed to stone:
I asked help of that which to help had no power,
    I sought love where love was utterly unknown.

Idolator I kneeled to an idol cut in rock!
    I might have slashed my flesh and drawn my heart's best blood:
The Granite God had felt no tenderness, no shock;
    My Baal had not seen nor heard nor understood.

In dark remorse I rose: I rose in darker shame;
    Self-condemned I withdrew to an exile from my kind;
A solitude I sought where mortal never came,
    Hoping in its wilds forgetfulness to find.

Now, Heaven, heal the wound which I still deeply feel;
    Thy glorious hosts look not in scorn on our poor race;
Thy King eternal doth no iron judgement deal
    On suffering worms who seek forgiveness, comfort, grace.

He gave our hearts to love: He will not love despise,
    E'en if the gift be lost, as mine was long ago;
He will forgive the fault, will bid the offender rise,
    Wash out with dews of bliss the fiery brand of woe;

And give a sheltered place beneath the unsullied throne,
    Whence the soul redeemed may mark Time's fleeting course
                                                round earth;
And know its trials overpast, its sufferings gone,
    And feel the peril past of Death's immortal birth.

On the Death of Emily Jane Brontë

My darling, thou wilt never know
The grinding agony of woe
   That we have borne for thee.
Thus may we consolation tear
E'en from the depth of our despair
   And wasting misery.

The nightly anguish thou art spared
When all the crushing truth is bared
   To the awakening mind,
When the galled heart is pierced with grief,
Till wildly it implores relief,
   But small relief can find.

Nor know'st thou what it is to lie
Looking forth with streaming eye
   On life's lone wilderness.
'Weary, weary, dark and drear,
How shall I the journey bear,
   The burden and distress?'

Then since thou art spared such pain
We will not wish thee here again;
   He that lives must mourn.
God help us through our misery
And give us rest and joy with thee
   When we reach our bourne!

On the Death of Anne Brontë

There's little joy in life for me,
   And little terror in the grave;
I've lived the parting hour to see
   Of one I would have died to save.

55

Calmly to watch the failing breath,
    Wishing each sigh might be the last;
Longing to see the shade of death
    O'er those belovēd features cast.

The cloud, the stillness that must part
    The darling of my life from me;
And then to thank God from my heart,
    To thank Him well and fervently;

Although I knew that we had lost
    The hope and glory of our life;
And now, benighted, tempest-tossed,
    Must bear alone the weary strife.

POEMS BY EMILY JANE BRONTË

'High waving heather, 'neath stormy blasts bending'

High waving heather, 'neath stormy blasts bending,
Midnight and moonlight and bright shining stars;
Darkness and glory rejoicingly blending,
Earth rising to heaven and heaven descending,
Man's spirit away from its drear dungeon sending,
Bursting the fetters and breaking the bars.

All down the mountain sides, wild forests lending
One mighty voice to the life-giving wind;
Rivers their banks in the jubilee rending,
Fast through the valleys a reckless course wending,
Wider and deeper their waters extending,
Leaving a desolate desert behind.

Shining and lowering and swelling and dying,
Changing for ever from midnight to noon;
Roaring like thunder, like soft music sighing,
Shadows on shadows advancing and flying,
Lightning-bright flashes the deep gloom defying,
Coming as swiftly and fading as soon.

'All day I've toiled, but not with pain'

All day I've toiled, but not with pain,
In learning's golden mine;
And now at eventide again
The moonbeams softly shine.

There is no snow upon the ground,
No frost on wind or wave;
The south wind blew with gentlest sound
And broke their icy grave.

'Tis sweet to wander here at night
To watch the winter die,

With heart as summer sunshine light
And warm as summer sky.

O may I never lose the peace
That lulls me gently now,
Though time should change my youthful face,
And years should shade my brow!

True to myself, and true to all,
May I be healthful still,
And turn away from passion's call,
And curb my own wild will.

'I am the only being whose doom'

I am the only being whose doom
No tongue would ask, no eye would mourn;
I never caused a thought of gloom,
A smile of joy, since I was born.

In secret pleasure, secret tears,
This changeful life has slipped away,
As friendless after eighteen years,
As lone as on my natal day.

There have been times I cannot hide,
There have been times when this was drear,
When my sad soul forgot its pride
And longed for one to love me here.

But those were in the early glow
Of feelings since subdued by care;
And they have died so long ago,
I hardly now believe they were.

First melted off the hope of youth,
Then fancy's rainbow fast withdrew;

And then experience told me truth
In mortal bosoms never grew.

'Twas grief enough to think mankind
All hollow, servile, insincere;
But worse to trust to my own mind
And find the same corruption there.

'Only some spires of bright green grass'

Only some spires of bright green grass
Transparently in sunshine quivering

'Now trust a heart that trusts in you'

Now trust a heart that trusts in you,
And firmly say the word 'Adieu';
Be sure, wherever I may roam,
My heart is with your heart at home;

Unless there be no truth on earth,
And vows meant true are nothing worth,
And mortal man have no control
Over his own unhappy soul;

Unless I change in every thought,
And memory will restore me nought,
And all I have of virtue die
Beneath far Gondal's foreign sky.

The mountain peasant loves the heath
Better than richest plains beneath;
He would not give one moorland wild
For all the fields that ever smiled;

And whiter brows than yours may be,
And rosier cheeks my eyes may see,
And lightning looks from orbs divine
About my pathway burn and shine;

But that pure light, changeless and strong,
Cherished and watched and nursed so long;
That love that first its glory gave
Shall be my pole star to the grave.

A. G. A.

Sleep brings no joy to me,
Remembrance never dies;
My soul is given to misery
And lives in sighs.

Sleep brings no rest to me;
The shadows of the dead
My waking eyes may never see
Surround my bed.

Sleep brings no hope to me;
In soundest sleep they come,
And with their doleful imagery
Deepen the gloom.

Sleep brings no strength to me,
No power renewed to brave,
I only sail a wilder sea,
A darker wave.

Sleep brings no friend to me
To soothe and aid to bear;
They all gaze, oh, how scornfully,
And I despair.

Sleep brings no wish to knit
My harassed heart beneath;
My only wish is to forget
In sleep of death.

'I'll come when thou art saddest'

I'll come when thou art saddest,
Laid alone in the darkened room;
When the mad day's mirth has vanished,
And the smile of joy is banished
From evening's chilly gloom.

I'll come when the heart's real feeling
Has entire, unbiased sway,
And my influence o'er thee stealing,
Grief deepening, joy congealing,
Shall bear thy soul away.

Listen, 'tis just the hour,
The awful time for thee;
Dost thou not feel upon thy soul
A flood of strange sensations roll,
Forerunners of a sterner power,
Heralds of me?

'I'm happiest when most away'

I'm happiest when most away
I can bear my soul from its home of clay
On a windy night when the moon is bright
And the eye can wander through worlds of light —

When I am not and none beside —
Nor earth nor sea nor cloudless sky —
But only spirit wandering wide
Through infinite immensity.

Song

King Julius left the south country
His banners all bravely flying;
His followers went out with Jubilee
But they shall return with sighing.

Loud arose the triumphal hymn
The drums were loudly rolling,
Yet you might have heard in distance dim
How a passing bell was tolling.

The sword so bright from battles won
With unseen rust is fretting,
The evening comes before the noon,
The scarce risen sun is setting.

While princes hang upon his breath
And nations round are fearing,
Close by his side a daggered death
With sheathless point stands sneering.

That death he took a certain aim,
For Death is stony-hearted
And in the zenith of his fame
Both power and life departed.

'And now the house-dog stretched once more'

And now the house-dog stretched once more
His limbs upon the glowing floor;
The children half resumed their play,
Though from the warm hearth scared away.
The goodwife left her spinning-wheel,
And spread with smiles the evening meal;
The shepherd placed a seat and pressed

To their poor fare his unknown guest.
And he unclasped his mantle now,
And raised the covering from his brow;
Said, 'Voyagers by land and sea
Were seldom feasted daintily';
And checked his host by adding stern
He'd no refinement to unlearn.
A silence settled on the room;
The cheerful welcome sank to gloom;
But not those words, though cold and high,
So froze their hospitable joy.
No — there was something in his face,
Some nameless thing they could not trace,
And something in his voice's tone
Which turned their blood as chill as stone.
The ringlets of his long black hair
Fell o'er a cheek most ghastly fair.
Youthful he seemed—but worn as they
Who spend too soon their youthful day.
When his glance drooped, 'twas hard to quell
Unbidden feelings' sudden swell;
And pity scarce her tears could hide,
So sweet that brow, with all its pride;
But when upraised his eye would dart
An icy shudder through the heart.
Compassion changed to horror then
And fear to meet that gaze again.
It was not hatred's tiger-glare,
Nor the wild anguish of despair;
It was not useless misery
Which mocks at friendship's sympathy.
No — lightning all unearthly shone
Deep in that dark eye's circling zone,
Such withering lightning as we deem
None but a spectre's look may beam;
And glad they were when he turned away
And wrapped him in his mantle grey,

Leant down his head upon his arm
And veiled from view their basilisk charm.

'Shed no tears o'er that tomb'

Shed no tears o'er that tomb
For there are Angels weeping;
Mourn not him whose doom
Heaven itself is mourning.
Look how in sable gloom
The clouds are earthward sweeping,
And earth receives them home,
Even darker clouds returning.

Is it when good men die
That sorrow wakes above?
Grieve saints when other spirits fly
To swell their choir of love?

Ah no, with louder sound
The golden harp-strings quiver
When good men gain the happy ground
Where they must dwell for ever.

But he who slumbers there,
His bark will strive no more
Across the waters of despair
To reach that glorious shore.

The time of grace is past
And mercy scorned and tried
Forsakes to utter wrath at last
The soul so steeled by pride.

That wrath will never spare,
Will never pity know,

Will mock its victim's maddened prayer,
Will triumph in his woe.

Shut from his Maker's smile
The accursed man shall be:
Compassion reigns a little while,
Revenge eternally.

A. A. A.

Sleep not, dream not; this bright day
Will not, cannot last for aye;
Bliss like thine is bought by years
Dark with torment and with tears.

Sweeter far than placid pleasure,
Purer, higher beyond measure,
Yet alas the sooner turning
Into hopeless, endless mourning.

I love thee, boy; for all divine,
All full of God thy features shine.
Darling enthusiast, holy child,
Too good for this world's warring wild,
Too heavenly now but doomed to be
Hell-like in heart and misery.

And what shall change that angel brow
And quench that spirit's glorious glow?
Relentless laws that disallow
True virtue and true joy below.

And blame me not, if, when the dread
Of suffering clouds thy youthful head,
If when by crime and sorrow tost
Thy wandering bark is wrecked and lost

I too depart, I too decline,
And make thy path no longer mine.
'Tis thus that human minds will turn,
All doomed alike to sin and mourn
Yet all with long gaze fixed afar,
Adoring virtue's distant star.

Song

O between distress and pleasure
Fond affection cannot be;
Wretched hearts in vain would treasure
Friendship's joys when others flee.

Well I know thine eye would never
Smile, while mine grieved, willingly;
Yet I know thine eye for ever
Could not weep in sympathy.

Let us part, the time is over
When I thought and felt like thee;
I will be an Ocean rover,
I will sail the desert sea.

Isles there are beyond its billow:
Lands where woe may wander free;
And, beloved, thy midnight pillow
Will be soft unwatched by me.

Not on each returning morrow
When thy heart bounds ardently
Need'st thou then dissemble sorrow,
Marking my despondency.

Day by day some dreary token
Will forsake thy memory
Till at last all old links broken
I shall be a dream to thee.

'There was a time when my cheek burned'

There was a time when my cheek burned
To give such scornful fiends the lie;
Ungoverned nature madly spurned
The law that bade it not defy.
O in the days of ardent youth
I would have given my life for truth.

For truth, for right, for liberty,
I would have gladly, freely died;
And now I calmly hear and see
The vain man smile, the fool deride;
Though not because my heart is tame,
Though not for fear, though not for shame.

My soul still chafes at every tone
Of selfish and self-blinded error;
My breast still braves the world alone,
Steeled as it ever was to terror;
Only I know, however I frown,
The same world will go rolling on.

' "Well, some may hate, and some may scorn" '

'Well, some may hate, and some may scorn,
And some may quite forget thy name,
But my sad heart must ever mourn
Thy ruined hopes, thy blighted fame.'

'Twas thus I thought, an hour ago,
Even weeping o'er that wretch's woe.
One word turned back my gushing tears,
And lit my altered eye with sneers.

'Then bless the friendly dust,' I said,
'That hides thy unlamented head.

Vain as thou wert, and weak as vain,
The slave of falsehood, pride and pain,
My heart has nought akin to thine —
Thy soul is powerless over mine.'

But these were thoughts that vanished too —
Unwise, unholy, and untrue —
Do I despise the timid deer
Because his limbs are fleet with fear?
Or would I mock the wolf's death-howl
Because his form is gaunt and foul?
Or hear with joy the leveret's cry
Because it cannot bravely die?

No! Then above his memory
Let pity's heart as tender be:
Say, 'Earth lie lightly on that breast,
And, kind Heaven, grant that spirit rest!'

'It is too late to call thee now'

It is too late to call thee now:
I will not nurse that dream again;
For every joy that lit my brow
Would bring its after-storm of pain.

Besides, the mist is half withdrawn;
The barren mountain-side lies bare;
And sunshine and awaking morn
Paint no more golden visions there.

Yet, ever in my grateful breast,
Thy darling shade shall cherished be;
For God alone doth know how blest
My early years have been in thee!

'Riches I hold in light esteem'

Riches I hold in light esteem
And Love I laugh to scorn
And lust of Fame was but a dream
That vanished with the morn —

And if I pray, the only prayer
That moves my lips for me
Is — 'Leave the heart that now I bear
And give me liberty.'

Yes, as my swift days near their goal
'Tis all that I implore —
Through life and death a chainless soul
With courage to endure!

'Shall Earth no more inspire thee'

Shall Earth no more inspire thee,
Thou lonely dreamer now?
Since passion may not fire thee
Shall Nature cease to bow?

Thy mind is ever moving
In regions dark to thee;
Recall its useless roving —
Come back and dwell with me.

I know my mountain breezes
Enchant and soothe thee still —
I know my sunshine pleases
Despite thy wayward will.

When day with evening blending
Sinks from the summer sky,

I've seen thy spirit bending
In fond idolatry.

I've watched thee every hour;
I know my mighty sway,
I know my magic power
To drive thy griefs away.

Few hearts to mortals given
On earth so wildly pine;
Yet none would ask a Heaven
More like this Earth than thine.

Then let my winds caress thee;
Thy comrade let me be —
Since nought beside can bless thee,
Return and dwell with me.

'Aye, there it is! It wakes to-night'

Aye, there it is! It wakes to-night
Sweet thoughts that will not die
And feeling's fires flash all as bright
As in the years gone by!

And I can tell by thine altered cheek
And by thy kindled gaze
And by the words thou scarce dost speak,
How wildly fancy plays.

Yes, I could swear that glorious wind
Has swept the world aside,
Has dashed its memory from thy mind
Like foam-bells from the tide —

And thou art now a spirit pouring
Thy presence into all —

The essence of the Tempest's roaring
And of the Tempest's fall —

A universal influence
From Thine own influence free;
A principle of life, intense,
Lost to mortality.

Thus truly when that breast is cold
Thy prisoned soul shall rise,
The dungeon mingle with the mould —
The captive with the skies.

How Clear She Shines!

How clear she shines! How quietly
I lie beneath her silver light
While Heaven and Earth are whispering me,
'To-morrow wake, but dream to-night.'

Yes, Fancy, come, my Fairy love!
These throbbing temples, softly kiss;
And bend my lonely couch above
And bring me rest and bring me bliss.

The world is going — Dark world, adieu!
Grim world, go hide thee till the day;
The heart thou canst not all subdue
Must still resist if thou delay!

Thy love I will not, will not share;
Thy hatred only wakes a smile;
Thy griefs may wound — thy wrongs may tear,
But, oh, thy lies shall ne'er beguile!

While gazing on the stars that glow
Above me in that stormless sea,

I long to hope that all the woe
Creation knows, is held in thee!

And this shall be my dream to-night —
I'll think the heaven of glorious spheres
Is rolling on its course of light
In endless bliss through endless years;

I'll think there's not one world above,
Far as these straining eyes can see,
Where Wisdom ever laughed at Love,
Or Virtue crouched to Infamy;

Where, writhing 'neath the strokes of Fate,
The mangled wretch was forced to smile;
To match his patience 'gainst her hate,
His heart rebellious all the while;

Where Pleasure still will lead to wrong,
And helpless Reason warn in vain;
And Truth is weak and Treachery strong,
And Joy the shortest path to Pain;

And Peace, the lethargy of grief;
And Hope, a phantom of the soul;
And Life, a labour void and brief;
And Death, the despot of the whole!

'In the earth, the earth, thou shalt be laid'

In the earth, the earth, thou shalt be laid,
A grey stone standing over thee;
Black mould beneath thee spread
And black mould to cover thee.

'Well, there is rest there,
So fast come thy prophecy;

The time when my sunny hair
Shall with grass roots twinèd be.'

But cold, cold is that resting place,
Shut out from Joy and Liberty,
And all who loved thy living face
Will shrink from its gloom and thee.

'Not so: *here* the world is chill,
And sworn friends fall from me;
But *there*, they'll own me still
And prize my memory.'

Farewell, then, all that love,
All that deep sympathy:
Sleep on; heaven laughs above,
Earth never misses thee.

Turf-sod and tombstone drear
Part human company;
One heart broke only there —
That heart was worthy thee!

A. G. A. to A. S.

This summer wind, with thee and me
Roams in the dawn of day;
But thou must be where it shall be,
Ere Evening — far away.

The farewell's echo from thy soul
Should not depart before
Hills rise and distant rivers roll
Between us evermore.

I know that I have done thee wrong —
Have wronged both thee and Heaven —

75

And I may mourn my lifetime long
Yet may not be forgiven.

Repentant tears will vainly fall
To cancel deeds untrue;
But for no grief can I recall
The dreary word — Adieu.

Yet thou a future peace shalt win
Because thy soul is clear;
And I who had the heart to sin
Will find a heart to bear.

Till far beyond earth's frenzied strife
That makes destruction joy,
Thy perished faith shall spring to life
And my remorse shall die.

'Come, walk with me'

Come, walk with me;
There's only thee
To bless my spirit now;
We used to love on winter nights
To wander through the snow.
Can we not woo back old delights?
The clouds rush dark and wild;
They fleck with shade our mountain heights
The same as long ago,
And on the horizon rest at last
In looming masses piled;
While moonbeams flash and fly so fast
We scarce can say they smiled.

Come, walk with me — come, walk with me;
We were not once so few;

But Death has stolen our company
As sunshine steals the dew:
He took them one by one, and we
Are left, the only two;
So closer would my feelings twine,
Because they have no stay but thine.

'Nay, call me not; it may not be;
Is human love so true?
Can Friendship's flower droop on for years
And then revive anew?
No; though the soil be wet with tears,
How fair soe'er it grew;
The vital sap once perishèd
Will never flow again;
And surer than that dwelling dread,
The narrow dungeon of the dead,
Time parts the hearts of men.'

To Imagination

When weary with the long day's care,
And earthly change from pain to pain,
And lost, and ready to despair,
Thy kind voice calls me back again —
O my true friend, I am not lone
While thou canst speak in such a tone!

So hopeless is the world without,
The world within I doubly prize;
Thy world where guile and hate and doubt
And cold suspicion never rise;
Where thou and I and Liberty
Have undisputed sovereignty.

What matters it that all around
Danger and grief and darkness lie,

If but within our bosom's bound
We hold a bright unsullied sky,
Warm with ten thousand mingled rays
Of suns that know no winter days?

Reason indeed may oft complain
For Nature's sad reality,
And tell the suffering heart how vain
Its cherished dreams must always be;
And Truth may rudely trample down
The flowers of Fancy newly blown.

But thou art ever there to bring
The hovering visions back and breathe
New glories o'er the blighted spring
And call a lovelier life from death,
And whisper with a voice divine
Of real worlds as bright as thine.

I trust not to thy phantom bliss,
Yet still in evening's quiet hour
With never-failing thankfulness
I welcome thee, benignant power,
Sure solacer of human cares
And brighter hope when hope despairs.

'O thy bright eyes must answer now'

O thy bright eyes must answer now,
When Reason, with a scornful brow,
Is mocking at my overthrow;
O thy sweet tongue must plead for me
And tell why I have chosen thee!

Stern Reason is to judgement come
Arrayed in all her forms of gloom:

Wilt thou my advocate be dumb?
No, radiant angel, speak and say
Why I did cast the world away;

Why I have persevered to shun
The common paths that others run;
And on a strange road journeyed on
Heedless alike of Wealth and Power —
Of Glory's wreath and Pleasure's flower.

These once indeed seemed Beings divine,
And they perchance heard vows of mine
And saw my offerings on their shrine —
But, careless gifts are seldom prized,
And mine were worthily despised;

So with a ready heart I swore
To seek their altar-stone no more,
And gave my spirit to adore
Thee, ever present, phantom thing —
My slave, my comrade, and my King!

A slave because I rule thee still;
Incline thee to my changeful will
And make thy influence good or ill —
A comrade, for by day and night
Thou art my intimate delight —

My Darling Pain that wounds and sears
And wrings a blessing out from tears
By deadening me to real cares;
And yet, a king — though prudence well
Have taught thy subject to rebel.

And am I wrong to worship where
Faith cannot doubt nor Hope despair
Since my own soul can grant my prayer?
Speak, God of Visions, plead for me
And tell why I have chosen thee!

The Philosopher's Conclusion

'Enough of Thought, Philosopher;
Too long hast thou been dreaming
Unlightened, in this chamber drear
While summer's sun is beaming —
Space-sweeping soul, what sad refrain
Concludes thy musings once again?

'O for the time when I shall sleep
Without identity,
And never care how rain may steep
Or snow may cover me!

'No promised Heaven, these wild Desires
Could all or half fulfil;
No threatened Hell, with quenchless fires,
Subdue this quenchless will!'

— So said I, and still say the same;
— Still to my Death will say —
Three Gods within this little frame
Are warring night and day.

Heaven could not hold them all, and yet
They all are held in me
And must be mine till I forget
My present entity.

O for the time when in my breast
Their struggles will be o'er;
O for the day when I shall rest,
And never suffer more!

'I saw a Spirit standing, Man,
Where thou dost stand — an hour ago;
And round his feet, three rivers ran
Of equal depth and equal flow —

80

'A Golden stream, and one like blood,
And one like Sapphire, seemed to be,
But where they joined their triple flood
It tumbled in an inky sea.

'The Spirit bent his dazzling gaze
Down on that Ocean's gloomy night,
Then — kindling all with sudden blaze,
The glad deep sparkled wide and bright —
White as the sun; far, far more fair
Than the divided sources were!'

— And even for that Spirit, Seer,
I've watched and sought my lifetime long;
Sought him in Heaven, Hell, Earth and Air,
An endless search — and always wrong!

Had I but seen his glorious eye
Once light the clouds that 'wilder me,
I ne'er had raised this coward cry
To cease to think and cease to be —

I ne'er had called oblivion blest,
Nor stretching eager hands to Death
Implored to change for lifeless rest
This sentient soul, this living breath.

O let me die, that power and will
Their cruel strife may close,
And vanquished Good, victorious Ill
Be lost in one repose.

R. Alcona to J. Brenzaida

Cold in the earth, and the deep snow piled above thee!
Far, far removed, cold in the dreary grave!
Have I forgot, my Only Love, to love thee,
Severed at last by Time's all-wearing wave?

Now, when alone, do my thoughts no longer hover
Over the mountains on Angora's shore;
Resting their wings where heath and fern-leaves cover
That noble heart for ever, ever more?

Cold in the earth, and fifteen wild Decembers
From those brown hills have melted into spring —
Faithful indeed is the spirit that remembers
After such years of change and suffering!

Sweet Love of youth, forgive if I forget thee
While the World's tide is bearing me along:
Sterner desires and darker hopes beset me,
Hopes which obscure but cannot do thee wrong.

No other Sun has lightened up my heaven;
No other Star has ever shone for me:
All my life's bliss from thy dear life was given —
All my life's bliss is in the grave with thee.

But when the days of golden dreams had perished
And even Despair was powerless to destroy,
Then did I learn how existence could be cherished,
Strengthened and fed without the aid of joy;

Then did I check the tears of useless passion,
Weaned my young soul from yearning after thine;
Sternly denied its burning wish to hasten
Down to that tomb already more than mine!

And even yet, I dare not let it languish,
Dare not indulge in Memory's rapturous pain;
Once drinking deep of that divinest anguish,
How could I seek the empty world again?

'Death, that struck when I was most confiding'

Death, that struck when I was most confiding
In my certain Faith of Joy to be,
Strike again, Time's withered branch dividing
From the fresh root of Eternity!

Leaves, upon Time's branch, were growing brightly,
Full of sap and full of silver dew;
Birds, beneath its shelter, gathered nightly;
Daily, round its flowers, the wild bees flew.

Sorrow passed and plucked the golden blossom,
Guilt stripped off the foliage in its pride;
But, within its parent's kindly bosom,
Flowed forever Life's restoring tide.

Little mourned I for the parted Gladness,
For the vacant nest and silent song;
Hope was there and laughed me out of sadness,
Whispering, 'Winter will not linger long.'

And behold, with tenfold increase blessing
Spring adorned the beauty-burdened spray;
Wind and rain and fervent heat caressing
Lavished glory on its second May.

High it rose; no wingèd grief could sweep it;
Sin was scared to distance with its shine:
Love and its own life had power to keep it
From all wrong, from every blight but thine!

Heartless Death, the young leaves droop and languish!
Evening's gentle air may still restore —
No: the morning sunshine mocks my anguish —
Time for me must never blossom more!

Strike it down, that other boughs may flourish
Where that perished sapling used to be;
Thus, at least, its mouldering corpse will nourish
That from which it sprung — Eternity.

'Ah! why, because the dazzling sun'

Ah! why, because the dazzling sun
Restored my earth to joy
Have you departed, every one,
And left a desert sky?

All through the night, your glorious eyes
Were gazing down in mine,
And with a full heart's thankful sighs
I blessed that watch divine!

I was at peace, and drank your beams
As they were life to me
And revelled in my changeful dreams
Like petrel on the sea.

Thought followed thought — star followed star
Through boundless regions on,
While one sweet influence, near and far,
Thrilled through and proved us one.

Why did the morning rise to break
So great, so pure a spell,
And scorch with fire the tranquil cheek
Where your cool radiance fell?

84

Blood-red he rose, and arrow-straight
His fierce beams struck my brow:
The soul of Nature sprang elate,
But mine sank sad and low!

My lids closed down — yet through their veil
I saw him blazing still;
And bathe in gold the misty dale,
And flash upon the hill.

I turned me to the pillow then
To call back Night, and see
Your worlds of solemn light, again
Throb with my heart and me!

It would not do — the pillow glowed
And glowed both roof and floor,
And birds sang loudly in the wood,
And fresh winds shook the door.

The curtains waved, the wakened flies
Were murmuring round my room,
Imprisoned there, till I should rise
And give them leave to roam.

O Stars and Dreams and Gentle Night;
O Night and Stars return!
And hide me from the hostile light
That does not warm, but burn —

That drains the blood of suffering men;
Drinks tears, instead of dew:
Let me sleep through his blinding reign,
And only wake with you!

'How beautiful the Earth is still'

How beautiful the Earth is still
To thee — how full of Happiness;
How little fraught with real ill
Or shadowy phantoms of distress;

How Spring can bring thee glory yet
And Summer win thee to forget
December's sullen time!
Why dost thou hold the treasure fast
Of youth's delight, when youth is past
And thou art near thy prime?

When those who were thy own compeers,
Equal in fortunes and in years,
Have seen their morning melt in tears,
To dull unlovely day;
Blest, had they died unproved and young
Before their hearts were wildly wrung,
Poor slaves, subdued by passions strong,
A weak and helpless prey!

'Because, I hoped while they enjoyed,
And by fulfilment, hope destroyed —
As children hope, with trustful breast,
I waited Bliss and cherished Rest.

'A thoughtful Spirit taught me soon
That we must long till life be done;
That every phase of earthly joy
Will always fade and always cloy —

'This I foresaw, and would not chase
The fleeting treacheries,
But with firm foot and tranquil face
Held backward from the tempting race,

Gazed o'er the sands the waves efface
To the enduring seas —

'There cast my anchor of Desire
Deep in unknown Eternity;
Nor ever let my Spirit tire
With looking for *What is to be*.

'It is Hope's spell that glorifies
Like youth to my maturer eyes
All Nature's million mysteries —
The fearful and the fair —

'Hope soothes me in the griefs I know,
She lulls my pain for others' woe
And makes me strong to undergo
What I am born to bear.

'Glad comforter, will I not brave
Unawed the darkness of the grave?
Nay, smile to hear Death's billows rave,
My Guide, sustained by thee?
The more unjust seems present fate
The more my Spirit springs elate
Strong in thy strength, to anticipate
Rewarding Destiny!'

from *Julian M. and A. G. Rochelle*

'Yet tell them, Julian, all, I am not doomed to wear
Year after year in gloom and desolate despair;
A messenger of Hope comes every night to me,
And offers, for short life, eternal liberty.

'He comes with western winds, with evening's wandering airs,
With that clear dusk of heaven that brings the thickest stars;

87

Winds take a pensive tone, and stars a tender fire,
And visions rise and change which kill me with desire —

'Desire for nothing known in my maturer years
When joy grew mad with awe at counting future tears;
When, if my spirit's sky was full of flashes warm,
I knew not whence they came, from sun or thunderstorm;

'But first a hush of peace, a soundless calm descends;
The struggle of distress and fierce impatience ends;
Mute music soothes my breast — unuttered harmony
That I could never dream till earth was lost to me.

'Then dawns the Invisible, the Unseen its truth reveals;
My outward sense is gone, my inward essence feels —
Its wings are almost free, its home, its harbour found;
Measuring the gulf it stoops and dares the final bound!

'Oh, dreadful is the check — intense the agony
When the ear begins to hear and the eye begins to see;
When the pulse begins to throb, the brain to think again,
The soul to feel the flesh and the flesh to feel the chain!

'Yet I would lose no sting, would wish no torture less;
The more that anguish racks the earlier it will bless;
And robed in fires of Hell, or bright with heavenly shine,
If it but herald Death, the vision is divine.'

'No coward soul is mine'

    No coward soul is mine
    No trembler in the world's storm-troubled sphere
    I see Heaven's glories shine
    And Faith stands equal arming me from Fear

    O God within my breast
    Almighty ever-present Deity

Life, that in me hast rest
As I Undying Life, have power in Thee

Vain are the thousand creeds
That move men's hearts, unutterably vain,
Worthless as withered weeds
Or idlest froth amid the boundless main

To waken doubt in one
Holding so fast by thy infinity
So surely anchored on
The steadfast rock of Immortality

With wide-embracing love
Thy spirit animates eternal years
Pervades and broods above,
Changes, sustains, dissolves, creates and rears

Though Earth and moon were gone
And suns and universes ceased to be
And thou wert left alone
Every Existence would exist in thee

There is not room for Death
Nor atom that his might could render void
Since thou art Being and Breath
And what thou art may never be destroyed.

'Why ask to know what date, what clime?'

Why ask to know what date, what clime?
There dwelt our own humanity,
Power-worshippers from earliest time,
Foot-kissers of triumphant crime
Crushers of helpless misery,
Crushing down Justice, honouring Wrong:
If that be feeble, this be strong.

Shedders of blood, shedders of tears:
Self-cursers avid of distress;
Yet mocking heaven with senseless prayers
For mercy on the merciless.

It was the autumn of the year
When grain grows yellow in the ear;
Day after day, from noon to noon,
The August sun blazed bright as June.

But we with unregarding eyes
Saw panting earth and glowing skies;
No hand the reaper's sickle held,
Nor bound the ripe sheaves in the field.

Our corn was garnered months before,
Threshed out and kneaded-up with gore;
Ground when the ears were milky sweet
With furious toil of hoofs and feet;
I, doubly cursed on foreign sod,
Fought neither for my home nor God.

Stanzas

Often rebuked, yet always back returning
  To those first feelings that were born with me,
And leaving busy chase of wealth and learning
  For idle dreams of things which cannot be:

To-day, I will not seek the shadowy region;
  Its unsustaining vastness waxes drear;
And visions rising, legion after legion,
  Bring the unreal world too strangely near.

I'll walk, but not in old heroic traces,
  And not in paths of high morality,

And not among the half-distinguished faces
The clouded forms of long-past history.

I'll walk where my own nature would be leading:
It vexes me to choose another guide:
Where the grey flocks in ferny glens are feeding;
Where the wild wind blows on the mountain side.

What have those lonely mountains worth revealing?
More glory and more grief than I can tell:
The earth that wakes one human heart to feeling
Can centre both the worlds of Heaven and Hell.

POEMS BY ANNE BRONTË

A Voice from the Dungeon

I'm buried now; I've done with life;
I've done with hate, revenge, and strife;
I've done with joy, and hope, and love,
And all the bustling world above.

Long have I dwelt forgotten here
In pining woe and dull despair,
This place of solitude and gloom
Must be my dungeon and my tomb,

No hope, no pleasure can I find;
I am grown weary of my mind;
Often in balmy sleep I try
To gain a rest from misery,

And in one hour of calm repose
To find a respite from my woes;
But dreamless sleep is not for me
And I am still in misery.

I dream of liberty 'tis true,
But then I dream of sorrow too,
Of blood and guilt and horrid woes,
Of tortured friends and happy foes;

I dream about the world, but then
I dream of fiends instead of men,
Each smiling hope so quickly fades
And such a lurid gloom pervades

That world — that when I wake and see,
Those dreary phantoms fade and flee,
Even in my dungeon I can smile,
And taste of joy a little while.

And yet it is not always so —
I dreamt a little while ago
That all was as it used to be,
A fresh free wind passed over me;

It was a pleasant summer's day,
The sun shone forth with cheering ray;
Methought a little lovely child
Looked up into my face and smiled.

My heart was full, I wept for joy,
It was my own, my darling boy.
I clasped him to my breast and he
Kissed me and laughed in childish glee.

Just then I heard in whisper sweet
A well known voice my name repeat.
His father stood before my eyes;
I gazed at him in mute surprise,

I thought he smiled and spoke to me,
But still in silent ecstasy
I gazed at him, I could not speak;
I uttered one long piercing shriek.

Alas! alas that cursed scream
Aroused me from my heavenly dream,
I looked around in wild despair
I called them, but they were not there,
The Father and the child are gone
And I must live and die alone!

Marina Sabia

The North Wind

That wind is from the North: I know it well;
   No other breeze could have so wild a swell.

Now deep and loud it thunders round my cell,
   Then faintly dies, and softly sighs,
And moans and murmurs mournfully.
I know its language: thus it speaks to me:

'I have passed over thy own mountains dear,
   Thy northern mountains, and they still are free;
Still lonely, wild, majestic, bleak and drear,
   And stern, and lovely, as they used to be

'When thou, a young enthusiast,
   As wild and free as they,
O'er rocks, and glens, and snowy heights,
   Didst often love to stray.

'I've blown the pure, untrodden snows
   In whirling eddies from their brows;
And I have howled in caverns wild,
Where thou, a joyous mountain-child,
   Didst dearly love to be.
The sweet world is not changed, but thou
Art pining in a dungeon now,
   Where thou must ever be.

'No voice but mine can reach thy ear,
And Heaven has kindly sent me here
   To mourn and sigh with thee,
And tell thee of the cherished land
   Of thy nativity.'

Blow on, wild wind; thy solemn voice,
   However sad and drear,
Is nothing to the gloomy silence
   I have had to bear.

Hot tears are streaming from my eyes,
   But these are better far

97

Than that dull, gnawing, tearless time,
  The stupor of despair.

Confined and hopeless as I am,
  Oh, speak of liberty!
Oh, tell me of my mountain home,
  And I will welcome thee!

Alexandrina Zenobia

Verses to a Child

Oh, raise those eyes to me again,
  And smile again so joyously;
And fear not, love; it was not pain
  Nor grief that drew those tears from me.
Belovèd child! thou canst not tell
The thoughts that in my bosom swell
  Whene'er I look on thee!

Thou knowest not that a glance of thine
  Can bring back long-departed years,
And that thy blue eyes' magic shine
  Can overflow my own with tears,
And that each feature, soft and fair,
And every curl of thy golden hair,
  Some sweet remembrance bears.

Just then thou didst recall to me
  A distant, long-forgotten scene;
One smile, and one sweet word from thee
  Dispelled the years that rolled between.
I was a little child again,
And every after joy and pain
  Seemed never to have been.

Tall forest trees waved over me
  To hide me from the heat of day,

And by my side a child like thee
　　Among the summer flowerets lay.
He was thy own, thou merry child:
Like thee he spoke, like thee he smiled,
　　Like thee he used to play.

Oh! those were calm and happy days;
　　We loved each other fondly then;
But human love too soon decays,
　　And ours can never bloom again.
I never thought to see the day
When Florian's friendship would decay
　　Like that of colder men.

Now, Flora, thou hast but begun
　　To sail on life's deceitful sea;
Oh! do not err as I have done,
　　For I have trusted foolishly
The faith of every friend I loved:
I never doubted till I proved
　　Their heart's inconstancy.

'Tis mournful to look back upon
　　Those long departed joys and cares,
And I *will* weep since thou alone
　　Art witness to my streaming tears.
This lingering love will not depart:
I cannot banish from my heart
　　The friend of childhood's years.

But though thy father loves me not,
　　Yet shall I still be loved by thee;
And, though I am by him forgot,
　　Say, wilt not thou remember me?
I will not cause *thy* heart to ache;
For thy regretted father's sake
　　I'll love and cherish thee.

Alexandrina Zenobia

Retirement

O let me be alone awhile:
　　No human form is nigh;
And I may sing and muse aloud,
　　No mortal ear is by.

Away! ye dreams of earthly bliss,
　　Ye earthly cares be gone:
Depart! ye restless wandering thoughts,
　　And let me be alone!

One hour, my spirit, stretch thy wings
　　And quit this joyless sod;
Bask in the sunshine of the sky,
　　And be alone with God!

Despondency

I have gone backward in the work,
　　The labour has not sped;
Drowsy and dark my spirit lies,
　　Heavy and dull as lead.

How can I rouse my sinking soul
　　From such a lethargy?
How can I break these iron chains
　　And set my spirit free?

There have been times when I have mourned
　　In anguish o'er the past,
And raised my suppliant hands on high,
　　While tears fell thick and fast;

And prayed to have my sins forgiven,
　　With such a fervent zeal,

An earnest grief — a strong desire,
That now I cannot feel.

And vowed to trample on my sins,
And called on Heaven to aid
My spirit in her firm resolves
And hear the vows I made.

And I have felt so full of love,
So strong in spirit then,
As if my heart would never cool,
Or wander back again.

And yet, alas! how many times
My feet have gone astray,
How oft have I forgot my God,
How greatly fallen away!

My sins increase, my love grows cold,
And Hope within me dies;
And Faith itself is wavering now;
Oh, how shall I arise?

I cannot weep, but I can pray,
Then let me not despair;
Lord Jesus, save me, lest I die;
Christ, hear my humble prayer!

To Cowper

Sweet are thy strains, celestial Bard;
And oft, in childhood's years,
I've read them o'er and o'er again,
With floods of silent tears.

The language of my inmost heart
I traced in every line;

My sins, *my* sorrows, hopes, and fears,
Were there — and only mine.

All for myself the sigh would swell,
The tear of anguish start;
I little knew what wilder woe
Had filled the Poet's heart.

I did not know the nights of gloom,
The days of misery;
The long, long years of dark despair,
That crushed and tortured thee.

But they are gone; from earth at length
Thy gentle soul is passed,
And in the bosom of its God
Has found its home at last.

It must be so, if God is love,
And answers fervent prayer;
Then surely thou shalt dwell on high,
And I may meet thee there.

Is He the source of every good,
The spring of purity?
Then in thine hours of deepest woe,
Thy God was still with thee.

How else, when every hope was fled,
Couldst thou so fondly cling
To holy things and holy men?
And how so sweetly sing

Of things that God alone could teach?
And whence that purity,
That hatred of all sinful ways —
That gentle charity?

Are *these* the symptoms of a heart
    Of heavenly grace bereft:
For ever banished from its God,
    To Satan's fury left?

Yet, should thy darkest fears be true,
    If Heaven be so severe,
That such a soul as thine is lost, —
    Oh! how shall *I* appear?

A Word to the 'Elect'

You may rejoice to think *yourselves* secure;
You may be grateful for the gift divine —
That grace unsought, which made your black hearts pure,
And fits your earth-born souls in Heaven to shine.

But, is it sweet to look around, and view
Thousands excluded from that happiness
Which they deserve at least as much as you —
Their faults not greater, nor their virtues less?

And, wherefore should you love your God the more,
Because to you alone His smiles are given;
Because He chose to pass the *many* o'er,
And only bring the favoured *few* to Heaven?

And, wherefore should your hearts more grateful prove,
Because for ALL the Saviour did not die?
Is yours the God of justice and of love?
And are your bosoms warm with charity?

Say, does your heart expand to all mankind?
And, would you ever to your neighbour do —
The weak, the strong, the enlightened, and the blind —
As you would have your neighbour do to you?

And, when you, looking on your fellow-men,
Behold them doomed to endless misery,
How can you talk of joy and rapture then? —
May God withhold such cruel joy from me!

That none deserve eternal bliss I know;
Unmerited the grace in mercy given:
But none shall sink to everlasting woe,
That have not well deserved the wrath of Heaven.

    And, oh! there lives within my heart
      A hope, long nursed by me;
    (And should its cheering ray depart,
      How dark my soul would be!)

    That as in Adam all have died,
      In Christ shall all men live;
    And ever round His throne abide,
      Eternal praise to give.

    That even the wicked shall at last
      Be fitted for the skies;
    And when their dreadful doom is past,
      To life and light arise.

    I ask not how remote the day,
      Nor what the sinners' woe,
    Before their dross is purged away;
      Enough for me, to know

    That when the cup of wrath is drained,
      The metal purified,
    They'll cling to what they once disdained,
      And live by Him that died.

Past Days

'Tis strange to think, there *was* a time
When mirth was not an empty name,
When laughter really cheered the heart,
And frequent smiles unbidden came,
And tears of grief would only flow
In sympathy for others' woe;

When speech expressed the inward thought,
And heart to kindred heart was bare,
And Summer days were far too short
For all the pleasures crowded there,
And silence, solitude, and rest,
Now welcome to the weary breast —

Were all unprized, uncourted then —
And all the joy one spirit showed,
The other deeply felt again;
And friendship like a river flowed,
Constant and strong its silent course,
For nought withstood its gentle force:

When night, the holy time of peace,
Was dreaded as the parting hour;
When speech and mirth at once must cease,
And Silence must resume her power;
Though ever free from pains and woes,
She only brought us calm repose.

And when the blessèd dawn again
Brought daylight to the blushing skies,
We woke, and not *reluctant* then,
To joyless *labour* did we rise;
But full of hope, and glad and gay,
We welcomed the returning day.

A Reminiscence

Yes, thou art gone! and never more
Thy sunny smile shall gladden me;
But I may pass the old church door,
And pace the floor that covers thee,

May stand upon the cold, damp stone,
And think that, frozen, lies below
The lightest heart that I have known,
The kindest I shall ever know.

Yet, though I cannot see thee more,
'Tis still a comfort to have seen;
And though thy transient life is o'er,
'Tis sweet to think that thou hast been;

To think a soul so near divine,
Within a form so angel fair,
United to a heart like thine,
Has gladdened once our humble sphere.

A Prayer

My God (oh, let me call Thee mine,
    Weak, wretched sinner though I be),
My trembling soul would fain be Thine;
    My feeble faith still clings to Thee.

Not only for the past I grieve,
    The future fills me with dismay;
Unless Thou hasten to relieve,
    Thy suppliant is a castaway.

I cannot say my faith is strong,
    I dare not hope my love is great;

But strength and love to Thee belong:
    Oh, do not leave me desolate!

I know I owe my all to Thee;
    Oh, take the heart I cannot give;
Do Thou my Strength, my Saviour be,
    And make me to Thy glory live!

Night

I love the silent hour of night,
    For blissful dreams may then arise,
Revealing to my charmèd sight
    What may not bless my waking eyes.

And then a voice may meet my ear,
    That death has silenced long ago;
And hope and rapture may appear
    Instead of solitude and woe.

Cold in the grave for years has lain
    The form it was my bliss to see;
And only dreams can bring again
    The darling of my heart to me.

Dreams

While on my lonely couch I lie,
    I seldom feel myself alone,
For fancy fills my dreaming eye
    With scenes and pleasures of its own.

Then I may cherish at my breast
    An infant's form beloved and fair;
May smile and soothe it into rest,
    With all a mother's fondest care.

How sweet to feel its helpless form
  Depending thus on me alone;
And while I hold it safe and warm,
  What bliss to think it is my own!

And glances then may meet my eyes
  That daylight never showed to me;
What raptures in my bosom rise
  Those earnest looks of love to see!

To feel my hand so kindly prest,
  To know myself beloved at last;
To think my heart has found a rest,
  My life of solitude is past!

But then to wake and find it flown,
  The dream of happiness destroyed;
To find myself unloved, alone,
  What tongue can speak the dreary void!

A heart whence warm affections flow,
  Creator, Thou hast given to me;
And am I only thus to know
  How sweet the joys of love would be?

If This be All

O God! if this indeed be all
  That Life can show to me;
If on my aching brow may fall
  No freshening dew from Thee,

If with no brighter light than this
  The lamp of hope may glow,
And I may only *dream* of bliss,
  And wake to weary woe;

If friendship's solace must decay,
    When other joys are gone,
And love must keep so far away,
    While I go wandering on, —

Wandering and toiling without gain,
    The slave of others' will,
With constant care and frequent pain,
    Despised, forgotten still;

Grieving to look on vice and sin,
    Yet powerless to quell
The silent current from within,
    The outward torrent's swell;

While all the good I would impart,
    The feelings I would share,
Are driven backward to my heart,
    And turned to wormwood there;

If clouds must *ever* keep from sight
    The glories of the Sun,
And I must suffer Winter's blight,
    Ere Summer is begun:

If Life must be so full of care,
    Then call me soon to Thee;
Or give me strength enough to bear
    My load of misery.

Song

We know where deepest lies the snow,
And where the frost-winds keenest blow
    On every mountain brow.
We long have known and learnt to bear

The wandering outlaw's toil and care,
But where we late were hunted, there
    Our foes are hunted now.

We have their princely homes, and they
To our wild haunts are chased away,
    Dark woods, and desert caves;
And we can range from hill to hill,
And chase our vanquished victors still,
Small respite will they find, until
    They slumber in their graves.

But I would rather be the hare
That, crouching in its sheltered lair,
    Must start at every sound;
That, forced from cornfields waving wide,
Is driven to seek the bare hillside,
Or in the tangled copse-wood hide,
    Than be the hunter's hound!

Song

Come to the banquet; triumph in your songs!
Strike up the chords, and sing of 'Victory!'
The oppressed have risen to redress their wrongs,
The Tyrants are o'erthrown, the Land is free!
The Land is free! Aye, shout it forth once more;
Is she not red with her oppressor's gore?

We are her champions; shall we not rejoice?
Are not the tyrants' broad domains our own?
Then wherefore triumph with a faltering voice?
And talk of freedom in a doubtful tone?
Have we not longed through life the reign to see
Of Justice, linked with Glorious Liberty?

Shout you that will, and you that can rejoice
To revel in the riches of your foes.
In praise of deadly vengeance lift your voice;
Gloat o'er your tyrants' blood, your victims' woes.
I'd rather listen to the skylark's songs,
And think on Gondal's and my father's wrongs.

It may be pleasant to recall the death
Of those beneath whose sheltering roof you lie;
But I would rather press the mountain-heath
With nought to shield me from the starry sky.
And dream of yet untasted victory —
A distant hope — and feel that I am free!

Oh, happy life! To range the mountains wild,
The waving woods, — or ocean's heaving breast,
With limbs unfettered, conscience undefiled,
And choosing where to wander, where to rest!
Hunted, opposed, but ever strong to cope
With toils and perils; ever full of hope!

'Our flower is budding.' When that word was heard
On desert shore, or breezy mountain's brow;
Wherever said, what glorious thoughts it stirred!
'Twas budding then; say, 'Has it blossomed now'
Is *this* the end we struggled to obtain?
Oh, for the wandering Outlaw's life again!

Oh, They Have Robbed Me of the Hope

Oh, they have robbed me of the hope
    My spirit held so dear;
They will not let me hear that voice
    My soul delights to hear.

They will not let me see that face
    I so delight to see;

111

And they have taken all thy smiles,
  And all thy love from me.

Well, let them seize on all they can —
  One treasure still is mine —
A heart that loves to think on thee,
  And feels the worth of thine.

Domestic Peace

Why should such gloomy silence reign,
  And why is all the house so drear,
When neither danger, sickness, pain,
  Nor death, nor want, has entered here?

We are as many as we were
  That other night, when all were gay
And full of hope, and free from care;
  Yet is there something gone away.

The moon without, as pure and calm,
  Is shining as that night she shone;
But now, to us, she brings no balm,
  For something from our hearts is gone.

Something whose absence leaves a void —
  A cheerless want in every heart;
Each feels the bliss of all destroyed,
  And mourns the change — but each apart.

The fire is burning in the grate
  As redly as it used to burn;
But still the hearth is desolate,
  Till mirth, and love, with *peace* return.

'Twas *peace* that flowed from heart to heart,
  With looks and smiles that spoke of heaven,

And gave us language to impart
  The blissful thoughts itself had given.

Domestic peace — best joy of earth!
  When shall we all thy value learn?
White angel, to our sorrowing hearth,
  Return, — oh, graciously return!

Severed and Gone

Severed and gone, so many years,
  And art thou still so dear to me,
That throbbing heart and burning tears
  Can witness how I clung to thee?

I know that in the narrow tomb
  The form I loved was buried deep,
And left in silence and in gloom
  To slumber out its dreamless sleep.

I know the corner where it lies
  Is but a dreary place of rest:
The charnel moisture never dries
  From the dark flagstones o'er its breast.

For there the sunbeams never shine,
  Nor ever breathes the freshening air:
But not for this do I repine,
  For my belovèd is not there.

Oh, no! I do not think of thee
  As festering there in slow decay:
'Tis this sole thought oppresses me,
  That thou art gone so far away.

For ever gone; for I, by night
  Have prayed, within my silent room,

That Heaven would grant a burst of light
    Its cheerless darkness to illume,

And give thee to my longing eyes
    A moment, as thou shinest now,
Fresh from thy mansion in the skies,
    With all its glory on thy brow.

Wild was the wish, intense the gaze
    I fixed upon the murky air,
Expecting, half, a kindling blaze
    Would strike my raptured vision there, —

A shape these human nerves would thrill,
    A majesty that might appal,
Did not thy earthly likeness still
    Gleam softly, gladly through it all.

False hope! vain prayer! It might not be
    That thou shouldst visit earth again;
I called on heaven — I called on thee —
    And watched, and waited, all in vain!

Had I one shining tress of thine,
    How would it bless these longing eyes!
Or if thy pictured form were mine,
    What gold should rob me of the prize?

A few cold words on yonder stone,
    A corpse as cold as they can be;
Vain words and mouldering dust, alone, —
    Can this be all that's left of thee?

Oh, no! thy spirit lingers still
    Where'er thy sunny smile was seen;
There's less of darkness, less of chill
    On earth, than if thou hadst not been.

Thou breathest in my bosom yet,
    And dwellest in my beating heart;
And while I cannot quite forget,
    Thou, darling, canst not quite depart.

Though freed from sin, and grief and pain,
    Thou drinkest now the bliss of Heaven,
Thou didst not visit earth in vain,
    And from us yet thou art not riven.

Life seems more sweet that thou didst live,
    And men more true that thou wert one;
Nothing is lost that thou didst give,
    Nothing destroyed that thou hast done.

Earth hath received thine earthly part;
    Thy heavenly flame hath heavenward flown;
But both still live within my heart
    Still live, and not in mine alone.

Farewell to Thee! But Not Farewell

Farewell to thee! but not farewell
    To all my fondest thoughts of thee:
Within my heart they still shall dwell;
    And they shall cheer and comfort me.

O beautiful, and full of grace!
    If thou hadst never met mine eye,
I had not dreamed a living face
    Could fancied charms so far outvie.

If I may ne'er behold again
    That form and face so dear to me,
Nor hear thy voice, still would I fain
    Preserve for aye their memory.

That voice, the magic of whose tone
  Could wake an echo in my breast,
Creating feelings that, alone,
  Can make my trancèd spirit blest.

That laughing eye, whose sunny beam
  My memory would not cherish less; —
And oh, that smile! whose joyous gleam
  No mortal language can express.

Adieu! but let me cherish still
  The hope with which I cannot part.
Contempt may wound, and coldness chill,
  But still it lingers in my heart.

And who can tell but Heaven, at last,
  May answer all my thousand prayers,
And bid the future pay the past
  With joy for anguish, smiles for tears.

Last Lines

A dreadful darkness closes in
  On my bewildered mind;
O let me suffer and not sin,
  Be tortured yet resigned.

Through all this world of blinding mist
  Still let me look to Thee,
And give me courage to resist
  The Tempter till he flee.

Weary I am, O give me strength
  And leave me not to faint;
Say Thou wilt comfort me at length
  And pity my complaint.

116

I've begged to serve Thee heart and soul,
    To sacrifice to Thee
No niggard portion, but the whole
    Of my identity.

I hoped amid the brave and strong
    My portioned task might lie,
To toil amid the labouring throng
    With purpose keen and high.

But Thou hast fixed another part,
    And Thou hast fixed it well;
I said so with my breaking heart
    When first the anguish fell.

O Thou hast taken my delight
    And hope of life away,
And bid me watch the painful night
    And wait the weary day.

The hope and the delight were Thine:
    I bless Thee for their loan;
I gave Thee while I deemed them mine
    Too little thanks I own.

Shall I with joy Thy blessings share
    And not endure their loss,
Or hope the martyr's Crown to wear
    And cast away the Cross?

These weary hours will not be lost,
    These days of passive misery,
These nights of darkness, anguish-tost,
    If I can fix my heart on Thee.

The wretch that weak and weary lies
    Crushed with sorrow, worn with pain,

Still to Heaven may lift his eyes
    And strive and labour not in vain.

That inward strife against the sins
    That ever wait on suffering
To strike wherever first begins
    Each ill that would corruption bring;

That secret labour to sustain
    With humble patience every blow;
To gather fortitude from pain
    And hope and holiness from woe.

Thus let me serve Thee from my heart
    Whate'er may be my written fate,
Whether thus early to depart
    Or yet a while to wait.

If Thou shouldst bring me back to life,
    More humbled I should be,
More wise, more strengthened for the strife,
    More apt to lean on Thee.

Should death be standing at the gate,
    Thus should I keep my vow,
But hard whate'er my future fate,
    So let me serve Thee now.

NOTES

Poems by Charlotte Brontë

'Lines Addressed to "The Tower of All Nations" '
The Tower of All Nations, deriving from the Tower of Babel, which
Charlotte Brontë had seen and marvelled at in a reproduction of
John Martin's spectacular picture, 'The Fall of Babylon', became an
important landmark in the Brontës' imaginary 'Glass Town'.

'Home-Sickness'
Lord Charles Wellesley is the protagonist of this poem. As Welling-
ton's son, his name held great glamour for Charlotte Brontë, and she
made him her pseudonym and hero in the early tales. It is note-
worthy that the Brontë sisters tended to assume male and not female
personae.

from 'Retrospection'
34 *Aaron's sceptre*: c.f. Numbers 17:8. Moses placed a stave from
each tribe in the Tabernacle overnight, to discover that only Aaron's
(representing the Levites) had 'put forth buds . . . and it bore ripe
almonds', indicating the special status of the priesthood and the
Levites.
44 *Sirius*: the dog-star which announces hot days in August.

'Turn not now for comfort here'
5 *Anvale*: probably territory in Angria.

'He could not sleep! — the couch of war'
22 *The Duke*: It seems likely that the poem concerns the return of
Zamorna, Charlotte Brontë's favourite and very Byronic hero, to
restore his rule in Angria.

'The Teacher's Monologue'
Manuscript dated May 1837, when Charlotte Brontë, teaching at
Roe Head, was at her lowest ebb, missing home and having received
a crushing letter from Southey advising her to abandon her dreams
of authorship.

'Gods of the Old Mythology'
2-4 *Adramalec* (Adrammelech): god of the Sepharvaim tribe in Samaria, to whom children were sacrificed. *Nergal*: Babylonian and Assyrian god of the underworld. *Anakim*: race of giants in Hebron descended from Anak. c.f. Numbers 13:3. *Argob*: an area of Syria.
15 *Ashtaroth* (Astarte): Semitic mother-goddess, worshipped especially in the capital of Bashan, Ashteroth-Karnaim.
19 *Semele*: daughter of Cadmus, beloved of Zeus.
26 *Moloch*: Ammonite god, to whom human sacrifice (especially children) was made.
31 *Dagon*: Philistine god, half man, half fish. 'Plague of the Philistine' because when the Philistines put the captured Ark of the Lord into his temple, they found next morning that 'Dagon was fallen upon his face to the ground . . . and the head of Dagon and both the palms of his hands were cut off upon the threshold.' c.f. I Samuel 4.
35 *Belial*: the spirit of iniquity.
41 *Mammon*: god of worldly commitment and cupidity.
56 *Thomas Aird*: one of the early contributors to *Blackwood's Magazine*.

'Preference'
Compare the theme of the idolized scholarly figure in this poem with the hero of 'Master and Pupil' (a poem whose sentimentality reflects the extremity of Charlotte's loneliness and frustration in adult life) and with Louis Moore in *Shirley* and M. Paul in *Villette*. Her heroines tend to prefer dominating, fatherly, and (often) middle-aged men.

Poems by Emily Jane Brontë

'A. G. A.' ('Sleep brings no joy to me')
Augusta Geraldine Almeda, the central Gondal heroine, having regained the throne of Gondal, finds her victory marred by guilt and loneliness.

'Song' ('King Julius left the south country')
Julius Brenzaida invades Gondal as claimant to the throne.

'And now the house-dog stretched once more'
Compare treatment of Heathcliff in *Wuthering Heights*, especially Chapters 4, 33 and 34.

'A. A. A.' ('Sleep not, dream not; this bright day')
Augusta again.

' "Well, some may hate, and some may scorn" '
This poem does not refer to the death of Branwell. The manuscript date is 1839: Branwell died nine years later. It is part of the Gondal cycle.

'Shall Earth no more inspire thee'
The existence of a poem such as this, which contradicts the visionary poet's rejection of the sensuous world, should warn one against too narrow a definition of Emily Brontë's philosophy.

'Aye, there it is!'
Charlotte Brontë's note to this poem is helpful: 'In these stanzas a louder gale has roused the sleeper on her pillow: the wakened soul struggles to blend with the storm by which it is swayed.'

'In the earth, the earth'
An example of the dialogue form which Emily Brontë frequently uses. The poem conducted as dialectic can achieve within itself an intellectual variety which also heightens its dramatic tension.

'A. G. A. to A. S.'
Augusta Geraldine Almeda is deserting her husband, Lord Alfred of Aspin Castle, for Julius Brenzaida.

'R. Alcona to J. Brenzaida'
Further to frustrate reason, the Gondal heroes often possess more than one name. Here, Augusta under the name of Rosina of Alcona, laments the death of the assassinated Julius Brenzaida.

from 'Julian M. and A. G. Rochelle'
The poem contains a total of 152 lines, and narrates in a somewhat

121

pedestrian fashion Julian's liberation of his enemy from prison. It cannot be precisely placed in the Gondal saga.

'Stanzas'
Some doubt has existed as to the authorship of this poem. Hatfield attributes it to Charlotte Brontë, attempting to restructure her dead sister's image along more conventionally acceptable lines. If so, it is Charlotte Brontë's finest poem. Yet the thought expressed in Emily's 'Shall Earth no more inspire thee' is not dissimilar.

Poems by Anne Brontë

'A Voice from the Dungeon'
Marina Sabia: unidentified Gondal heroine.

'The North Wind'
Alexandrina Zenobia: unidentified Gondal heroine.

'To Cowper'
c.f. Charlotte Brontë's novel, *Shirley*, whose heroines, Shirley Keeldar and Caroline Helstone, are thought to be based on the characters of Emily and Anne Brontë respectively. In Chapter 12, Caroline, speaking of Cowper's 'The Castaway', says: 'But he found relief in writing it — I know he did; and that gift of poetry — the most divine bestowed on man — was, I believe, granted to allay emotions when their strength threatens harm.'

'A Word to the "Elect"'
This poem was published in *The Universalist*, which reflected the views of a sect named the Beroen Universalists, a small group believing in the salvation of all. Anne Brontë corresponded with Rev. David Thom, who led the sect.

'If This be All'
For another example of Anne Brontë's unsentimental recognition that suffering does not always conduce to virtue, compare verse 6 with *The Tenant of Wildfell Hall*, Chapters 30 and 31.

'Domestic Peace'
Dated 'Monday Night, May 11, 1846'. It could refer to Branwell's disruption of the family peace at this period.

'Last Lines'
Dated 7 January 1849, less than three weeks after Emily Brontë's death, and the day after Anne had learnt from the doctor that her own disease was incurable.